THERE'S NO SUCH WORD AS CAN'T

BY EMMA SHEARDOWN

TURQUOISE

TIGER PRESS

Published by Turquoise Tiger Press, Lincolnshire, UK

Manufactured in the United Kingdom.

ISBN: 978-1-7398221-0-1

Table of Contents

Foreword by Taz Thornton v

Preface: Gold xi

Chapter 1: Fighting To Live 1

Chapter 2: Lady Di, Dusty Bin And My First Steps 5

Chapter 3: Legacy, Lambing and Life On The Farm 23

Chapter 4: Taking To The Saddle 29

Chapter 5: Schools, Bras and Animal Magic 37

Chapter 6: Mary, Uni, Hello Para Dressage 49

Chapter 7: Fairy and The Syston Flock 53

Chapter 8: Dad 63

Chapter 9: The Perfect Partnership 75

Chapter 10: Going For Gold 89

Chapter 11: World Champions 97

Chapter 12: Action Stations and More Medals 113

Chapter 13: Paralympic Dreams 119

Chapter 14: Wolfie 127

Chapter 15: Crashing, Netty and New Opportunities 137

Chapter 16: New Ambitions 147

Chapter 17: Emma: Pat's Story 153

Chapter 18: My Horses 159

Chapter 19: Teachers For All Of Us 161

Chapter 20: One Final Thought 163

Acknowledgements 167

For Dad

Thank you for all the love, support and opportunities
you gave me during our time together.

This time was cut far too short and whilst we both loved and
supported each other during our toughest times, in between we
made some amazing memories – memories I talk about
here and that I will always treasure.

I remember reading with you as a child. I always hated reading so
you would read with me and we would both read alternate pages.
I always made sure I got the half pages to read and
you read the full ones.

For this reason, I think the writing of this book would
have been a surprise to you just as it has been to
everybody else who knows me.

And it is for this reason I am dedicating this book to you.

Thank you, Dad for making all this possible.

— Emma

X

FOREWORD
by Taz Thornton

The first time I met Emma Sheardown, I fell foul of some of the biggest teachings she shares.

Emma's always grabbing every opportunity to tell the world and her wife not to dis ability in disability and yet, that's exactly what I did that day - in thought, if not in deed.

I saw Em wobble (to use her word) into a business networking event, accompanied by her mum, and wondered who she was and what her business might be.

Later, when we all gave our 40 second introductions, Emma slowly, and determinedly, announced that she had quadriplegic cerebral palsy and wanted to be a motivational speaker.

With the immense benefit of hindsight, I'm ashamed to admit my thoughts went something like this: 'How can she be a motivational speaker when she has trouble speaking?'

Perhaps not surprisingly, I wasn't the only one to have that thought. A couple of other well-meaning networkers asked me similar questions, and, because they knew me as a professional speaker and speaker coach, wondered if I might be able to help her achieve her aims.

Over the next few months, our paths crossed several times. Emma asked me for a few 1-1 sit downs in the breakout sessions at those networking events and my admiration for this remarkable young woman grew from strength to strength.

Before long, I'd worked out that Emma's speech patterns and movements were often adversely impacted by her levels of anxiety or stress. I can't even begin to imagine how nervous she must have been at that first networking event - standing up, in a room full of strangers, announcing her desire to become a professional speaker, complete with the knowledge that her first time fears would likely be cramping her delivery.

I noticed a real change as Emma's confidence grew. The more she relaxed in those 1-1 meetings, the easier her speech and movement became and the more I realised Emma had magic flowing through her veins and the very real potential to change lives - not only with her story, but with her passion, her determination and her unapologetic bloody mindedness. When this woman sets her mind on something, you can be sure she'll achieve it and then some. Tell Emma Sheardown she can't and it's like rocket fuel to her - I promise you, she'll go all out to prove you wrong!

And so, when Emma asked if I would become her coach and mentor, I was delighted to take on the challenge with her and do my absolute best to help her achieve her aims.

Emma is passionate, enthusiastic and a fast learner. The more she got out there and spoke in front of people, the more her confidence grew and the better she became. In no time at all, she utterly blew me away.

I'm not too proud to admit that working with Emma has provided me with many life lessons as well - not least not to dis ability in disability.

Actually, that's not entirely true; it was never about dissing ability for me - it was sheer ignorance and misunderstanding.

I had no idea of Emma's abilities - and I had no idea of what her limitations might be either.

Like so many, I didn't want to offend by asking the wrong questions, so fell into that trap of making assumptions - it's a safety bubble so many of us 'able bodied' people wrap ourselves in and, until someone like Emma bowls into our lives with a large pin, those bubbles go unchecked.

I'm so, so glad she burst mine! I'm even more delighted that, by writing this amazing debut book, she'll likely obliterate yours too!

Emma and I have now been working together as coach and coachee for a few years and, in the interests of fairness and transparency, it's only right that I present a full and accurate picture for you all.

I don't want you to read this and get some notion that my foreword might be a saccharine view of some superhero disability crusader who can never put a foot wrong!

Emma is remarkable in so many ways, but she *is* also human.

To use a colloquialism, Emma can sometimes 'spit the dummy' if things don't quite go to plan, and I'd be lying if I said I'd never asked if she needed a bit of mardy cream in the midst of a Sheardown-shaped tantrum!

Emma is way too hard on herself at times; she's stubborn, her own worst critic and, occasionally, hair-pullingly frustrating.

I've come to learn that kid gloves are not the best tool to help Emma come to her senses and realise she's perhaps, taking things way out of proportion. A bit of not-quite-brutal honesty, coupled with a bit of humour usually does the trick.

Once Em can see the futility of her tango with perfectionism and self-criticism, she's fast to learn from her *perceived* faux pas and turn them into learnings for future growth.

We've found a level of mutual respect and friendship that allows both of us to, at times, poke a little fun at one another and always come out laughing.

I'm not sure what anyone else would have thought had they heard our conversations about Emma attempting high fives, or her occasionally appearing to be swatting away a non-existent wasp when her arms respond in excitement over a new talk idea or animated discussion, but we've found our level and it works.

Emma always gives as good as she gets. I've learned that the absolute worst thing to do is try to pretend her CP doesn't exist - it's integral to Em's make up and part of what makes her such an amazing role model for so many.

If Emma can defy the medics, who feared she'd never walk or talk, by going on to bring home gold para dressage medals for her country AND become a professional motivational speaker, what's our excuse?

When it comes to excuses, there's something else we've been known to end up laughing about. Emma's often known to say "My arms and legs might not work as they should, but there's nothing wrong with my brain!" - and that's spot on... she's usually the sharpest tool in the box when it comes to everything from speaking up on equality and disability rights or making a witty retort.

...and that's precisely why I'll have none of it when she laughs and tries to use 'brain damage' as an excuse for not getting on with some of the coaching tasks we've set, or becoming so excited about one area of growing her brand and business that she conveniently 'forgets' something equally important that doesn't interest her quite as much!

Oh, how we laugh... and so does Emma's mum, who will usually remind her that she's 'forgotten' to do her share of washing the dishes as well.

So, there you have it. Emma Sheardown. Horrendously self-critical. Appallingly stubborn. Prone to chasing squirrels if we let her get away with it. Brilliantly driven. Wonderfully humorous. Sharp. Dedicated. Compassionate. Caring. Determined. And one of THE most inspiring speakers I've ever had the pleasure of coaching.

I'm so, so glad I didn't allow those initial fears and ignorances to prevent me from taking the time to get to know Emma. She's achieved so much in such a relatively short space of time, and she's taught me a ridiculous amount as well.

From organising an 'Audience With Emma Sheardown' event in a village hall to build her confidence, which resulted in a room full of people being moved to tears by her amazing story, to preparing Emma for some of her first, and major, platform speaking events, to watching her get a standing ovation for her first TEDx talk and encouraging her to go for it and deliver disability awareness training for Vodafone, this remarkable young woman has made me prouder and prouder.

It's not Emma's medals that make her solid gold - it's her attitude, and that's something we can ALL learn from.

Emma... you are one in a million and I cannot wait to see what the future holds for you AND all the people whose lives you'll positively touch.

This book is, I'm sure, the first of many brave steps towards inspiring a world of people who need some of that Sheardown magic in their lives. Look at you! You've done it - and there's so much more to come.

Keep on unleashing your awesome - you show us all there's no such word as can't!

Taz

X

GOLD

As my name was called out and I stepped forward onto the podium, I felt an overwhelming sense of pride that I had taken gold for my country. Seeing the Union flag raised and hearing the national anthem played sent goosebumps down my spine and brought a little tear to my eye. I was literally on top of the world.

Like any pony mad child I had looked up to the equestrian stars with hopes, dreams and ambitions, but, up until this moment, however much I dared to dream, there was a tiny part of me that had always felt this couldn't really be 'my' reality.

How wrong could I be? On 10th October, 2010 here I was collecting gold at the World Equestrian Games. World Number 1 in my class. I felt incredible.

Sharing the podium with GB team mates, Anne Durham and Sophie Christiansen, we had achieved a clean sweep of the medals. We had done it! I had done it!

This pony mad girl from Lincolnshire, the girl born with spastic quadriplegic cerebral palsy, who wasn't expected to live past her first two days of life, had not only survived against the odds but thrived, and here was the living proof: Emma Sheardown - World Champion.

CHAPTER 1

FIGHTING TO LIVE

Me, aged 9 months, with 'Big Ted'

The first of many challenges I was to face came at the very beginning of my life. On Tuesday 29th January 1985 - the day I was born.

My arrival, at Grantham Hospital, Lincolnshire, England, was traumatic.

Mum was admitted on the Monday and it was decided she would be induced on Tuesday. Dad had gone home briefly and on returning discovered Mum was about to have an emergency caesarean section. I was suffering with foetal distress. During birth, I was starved of oxygen which resulted in brain damage.

I spent the first few days of my life in an incubator in special baby care and was wired to various monitors, including a heart monitor. At two days' old doctors did not expect me to live.

One night, fearing the worst, a doctor phoned Dad, explained the situation and asked if he wanted me to be christened. If so the christening would need to take place straight away. Dad went to the hospital to be with me. I can't imagine the sheer worry, panic and upset, especially as on arrival he couldn't get in.

I am writing this with a tear in my eye as Dad must have felt so scared and alone. At the hospital, everywhere was locked, which must have added to his panic. Eventually Dad managed to get in thanks to a night porter who came to his rescue. He made it just in time to see me christened.

Oh, the irony. Twenty-seven years later and the tables would turn. It would be me rushing to hospital to see Dad, gravely ill. Heartbreakingly, I didn't get there in time and my dad passed away after a long illness.

In my first few days of life, Mum didn't know anything about the events during the night. She remembers waking up about 1am to go to the bathroom and noticing some flowers were missing out of the vase at the side of the bed. Thinking she must have been mistaken, she went back to sleep. The next morning the ward sister went into her carrying some flowers and told her about my christening.

I survived the night and remained in special baby care. Although I was still on the heart monitor, I slowly began to show signs of improvement. Mum told me that if she didn't believe in miracles before my christening, she did then. This seemed to be the point where I began to fight for myself without the aid of any monitors.

After three days, I was taken off the heart monitor. Mum was eventually discharged from hospital but allowed to stay with me. After 10 days, I was allowed home.

The first few weeks at home were far from plain sailing. The main problem was with feeding. In hospital Mum had to express her milk so it could be given to me, first of all, by tube and then by bottle so I never took to being breast fed. I suppose Mum had to be patient or I would have starved.

I remained in the care of the heart specialist for the first two to three months before I was finally discharged.

My development during those months appeared to progress slowly. I was beginning to take notice of things and noises around me and I smiled a lot, but my limbs were very tight and stiff.

My hands were always in a clenched fist. Mum had to prise my fingers open so she could wash my hands but, straight away, they went back into clenched fists. My head was very floppy and when laying down or being cuddled I went into the foetal position.

As time went by there were stages of my life that didn't happen. I couldn't roll over, I couldn't sit up and I didn't show any signs of crawling.

My maternal grandmother was worried about my very slow development. Whilst she found it difficult to talk to Mum about it she did talk to my mum's sisters, aunties, Christine and Barbara. They talked to my parents but they told me they thought Mum was in denial and Dad thought I was 'just slow'.

By the time I was a year old, I was still unable to roll over on my own and needed help to do so. I could only sit up if someone was behind me and supported me or I was well padded with cushions.

My parents had taken me back to the doctor's and shared their concerns. Our family doctor referred us to a paediatrician.

At 14 months old, I went to a specialist unit at the City Hospital in Nottingham for an assessment. Over a period of days I had x-rays, lumbar puncture, physio and speech therapy and various hand–eye co-ordination tests.

After my fourth visit I was diagnosed with Spastic Quadriplegic Cerebral Palsy (CP). This affected all four limbs, my balance and speech. My parents were told I wouldn't walk or talk.

Mum told me that after this diagnosis both she and Dad walked around the hospital grounds in silence and were both thinking the same. What is cerebral palsy? The specialist had explained it all and how it could affect me but the one thing that kept going through their heads was 'she won't walk and she won't talk'.

It must have been a huge shock.

Cerebral Palsy. So, what is it exactly? Let's make things nice and clear from the start. Cerebral Palsy is caused by a problem with the brain that occurs before, during or soon after birth. It can be the result of the brain either being damaged or not developing properly.

In my case, Mum had to have an emergency caesarean section because I was distressed in the womb and was temporarily starved of oxygen to the brain.

Cerebral Palsy is a group of permanent movement disorders that appear in early childhood. These disorders can vary. It's often said there are no two people with the same Cerebral Palsy.

My symptoms were and still are poor co-ordination, stiff muscles or high muscle tone, involuntary movements, balance and slight speech problems. Initially I also had difficulty with swallowing.

Often babies with Cerebral Palsy do not roll over, sit up, crawl or walk as early as other children of a similar age. These are all things I experienced.

There is no cure for Cerebral Palsy, but physiotherapy and other therapies such as speech and occupational therapy can help people develop and become more independent.

Spasticity is a form of hypertonia or increased muscle tone which results in stiff muscles. This can make movement difficult, if not impossible.

As I said before, all four of my limbs are affected. I have poor control and spasticity in both my arms and legs.

As you read my story you will learn how all these things have affected me throughout my life and continue to do so today.

I hope I can shed some light on what it's like living with CP and how it's possible to overcome challenges and live life to the full.

CHAPTER 2

LADY DI, DUSTY BIN AND MY FIRST STEPS

A very proud moment. Presenting flowers to Princess Diana, St Francis School, March, 1992. Pic courtesy of Lincolnshire Echo.

After my diagnosis, then came years of physiotherapy, occupational, speech therapy, work with a portage worker and regular appointments with my paediatrician.

Initially I saw physiotherapist, Liz Kendall, twice a week. She worked on my arms and legs as my muscles were very tight. Like most 15-month-old babies, I wanted to be on my feet but I wasn't allowed to weight bare because of the stiffness and lack of strength in my legs.

At this stage, my 'default' position was in the foetal position. I suppose I was a bit like a coiled spring in that, through doing my exercises or massaging me, Mum could straighten my body, my limbs or my fingers out. However, it wouldn't be long before I would concertina back into a small, tight ball.

Being so 'curled' up and tight, along with the weakness in my legs, meant even though I wanted to get on my feet and walk, my legs were not yet strong enough to support my body.

Only recently I experienced a similar situation. On a hot summer's day in 2019 all the muscles behind my knee and down my leg tightened up. My muscles were so tight I could not straighten my leg, let alone weight bare. It basically took me off my legs for about a week. I needed help to get around and was confined to my wheelchair. I was conscious of Mum having to lift me in and out of the chair which was not easy for her. I even bought myself a walking frame and gradually, with the use of the frame along with some exercises, got myself back on my feet.

This was a reminder of Mum talking about how my muscles had reacted as a baby. I can imagine the discomfort of her trying to straighten my leg on that day. It was a familiar discomfort that I felt all those years ago.

In terms of exercises as a young child, everything was done in stages. Seeing Liz was only part of the treatment. Mum and Dad had to put the programme into practice at home and this meant doing exercises several times a day, each session lasting about 20 minutes. Sometimes my aunties would give Mum and Dad a break and do the exercises with me.

Mum, Dad or my aunties, would manipulate my arms and legs to encourage movement and to get them to straighten. I would have to go through this regime four or five times a day and, during each session, Mum would work on my legs for five minutes and my arms for five minutes.

I can't remember whether these exercises hurt or not. However, from the spasms and muscle tightness I experience at times now, I can see these exercises would involve the same level of discomfort. It's caused by me trying to work against what my body naturally wants to do.

As time went by, my exercises developed and would start to incorporate things such as teaching me to roll over. Mum would place my arms and legs where they needed to be for me to be able to turn and then she would help and encourage me to roll the rest of the way.

I hated having to do my exercises. They were very uncomfortable at times and they were extremely boring. I wanted to play, I wanted to walk. Even at that age, there was something about doing so many exercises every day that seemed so time consuming and would frustrate me. Of course, at that early age, I didn't know or understand why I was being made to do them. That came later and with it, the rebellion.

My exercise regimes were so boring, sometimes they'd result in a real battle of wills with more than the odd tantrum thrown in as I tried to get out of them.

If I was tired or just simply 'not in the mood', then I would rebel.

My rebellion took the form of crying or shouting 'no' followed by some verbal outburst which was unintelligible. You could say I just kicked and screamed. I wasn't in any position to go and hide if I didn't want to do them. For one thing, I wasn't quick enough to escape.

I was either talked into doing the exercises or bribed. The bribe was either a sweet, a piece of chocolate or a biscuit, but not until the exercise was complete.

I can't remember how old I was when I realised how important my exercises were to my physical development. I think it was more a case of just accepting that this was part of my life.

Fortunately, despite me rebelling, my parents never gave in.

Nowadays, if I don't do some form of exercise then I get very stiff. It is important that I walk to keep my hips moving, although this may be a short distance. I have an exercise bike that I use most days as well as a machine to help my core strength.

Alongside physio I also had sessions with the occupational therapist (OT). My OT would work on my fine motor skills. As my hands were always in a clenched fist, my OT and Mum would straighten my fingers out and massage them to encourage them to open. They would also use different types of toys or puzzles like large, wooden puzzles with knobs on, to encourage me to use my fingers. These activities continued for quite some time.

Then I was encouraged to use a spoon or hold a beaker. Aged around three or four, fastening buttons, zips and shoe laces came into the equation. These are things I have difficulty with today, particularly buttons and zips on jeans, they are still a nightmare.

I also remember having a rag doll that Mum bought me from the Early Learning Centre. This doll was brightly coloured - the face, hands, hair, shoes, clothes, etc. were all different colours, so this was used to teach me colours. But it also had big buttons on the coat, a large zip on the trousers and laces on the shoes which I could practice doing up and undoing.

Even today, zips, buttons and shoe laces are still a challenge.

My parents were also concerned about my lack of speech – I will talk about this later.

At nine months Mum took me to a mother and baby swimming group. I enjoyed the freedom and, because my cousin Rachel went with us, loved splashing with her. I must say swimming is not something I enjoy doing now. Somewhere along the way I developed a fear of water.

Working alongside my physio, OT and speech therapists, was my portage worker, Diane Cudmore.

Portage is a home teaching scheme for pre-school children and began in a town in Wisconsin, USA. The scheme then came to this country in 1976.

Portage aims to work with families to help them develop a quality of life and experience for themselves and their young children in which they can "learn together, play together, participate and be included in their community in their own right".

Diane would discuss with my other therapists what area they would like me to work on. The idea of my portage sessions was to allow me to play but, whilst I was playing, it would include all the work I was doing with my therapists in my various programmes - a fun way of doing my exercises.

For example, if Diane was teaching me how to drink out of a cup I would practise picking up an empty cup and putting it down again, and how to drink out of it. I would try to say words like 'cup, drink, please and thank you', although I used to say 'ta', as I think 'thank you' was too complicated. The physio side of it would be sitting up unsupported.

My Uncle Alan made me a wooden, white desk and stool for me to sit at and do my portage work. He made it with sides so it gave me extra support and prevented me from falling sideways. The stool was measured and made to my height as it was very important I could sit comfortably and correctly with my back to a wall for support.

My feet needed to be flat to develop my balance and my posture. Even now if my feet are not firmly placed on a flat surface then my balance is severely affected. When I am riding, I need to have the feel of the stirrups under my feet.

When I was sat at the desk, Mum and Dad would get me to play with toys, do puzzles or have fun with Play-Doh - all of which encouraged me to use my hands and fingers.

I used the stool and desk for various stages of my development until I grew out of them. The stool went onto various other roles and I would sit on it to do different activities and exercises.

Diane would give Mum and Dad ideas of play exercises that they could do with me throughout the week.

Once a week I went to a play group at Grantham Health Clinic. This was basically a group portage play group which allowed me to interact with other children with similar disabilities. All the therapists would be there. We would play games, sing songs and do the hand movements and then we would have a drink and biscuits.

Our mums would usually disappear into another room, have coffee and a chat, and support one another.

All my therapy sessions were held at the clinic. It was opened in 1987 by HRH Princess of Wales and Mum and I were lucky enough to be invited on opening day. I was only two-and-a-half and so don't remember anything about it, if I'm honest. However, I do have a lovely photograph of Princess Diana kneeling, watching me walking on the parallel bars, as well as one of her stroking my face.

Mum remembers the day Princess Diana came very clearly. Everyone was very excited about the visit. There were six children in the portage playgroup and each child was doing a different activity.

Mum recalls the Princess asking her about my exercises and how they were helping my development. The royal visitor then asked Mum how she found doing the exercises with me.

The Princess was lovely. She had so much time for the children and their parents, remembers Mum.

Now I want to share with you some insights into the challenges of movement. I think it's important to explain some of the difficulties I have had to overcome in doing what many able-bodied people may find very easy to do.

Rolling Over

I was a long time mastering the art of rolling over. If I woke during the night either Mum or Dad would have to turn me over to reposition me and make me more comfortable as I was unable to roll myself over in bed.

Some nights I would only have to be rolled over a couple of times, whilst other nights, if I was unwell or unsettled, I needed rolling more frequently.

If they were playing with me on the floor I was unable to roll on to my tummy or my back so they had to help me. They placed my arms and legs in a position where, with encouragement, I could roll over. I can remember struggling to turn over.

Even now, rolling over is a struggle. I am not at all lady-like as it takes a huge amount of effort and adjusting myself. I suppose it is like doing a 90-point turn whilst rolling. This is all down to my lack of co-ordination.

Crawling

Can you imagine trying to teach someone to crawl when they have a lack of co-ordination in all four limbs and don't understand what's expected?

Well, this was another stage of development that had to be worked on and so my physio arranged for me to have a crawler.

The crawler was like a low stool, about six inches high and on four wheels. I would be laid on my tummy over the crawler and Mum and Dad, or whoever was about, would work together - one moving my arms and the other my legs.

According to Mum, one of them would crawl first so they got the co-ordination right in their minds.

I am not sure how long they did this for, but I was quite happy laid across the crawler. It was soft leather, well-padded and quite comfortable.

Eventually I got fed up. Learning to crawl properly just took so long as I couldn't co-ordinate my arms and legs correctly at a speed I wanted to move at.

This was when I adopted 'bunny-hopping' – a much quicker option, with no real co-ordination needed. I just knelt on the floor and pulled myself along with my arms.

Nowadays, I don't get down on the floor if I can help it as my hips just won't take it. However, on occasions where I do need to get down, I still 'bunny-hop' as I have never mastered the art of crawling.

Walking

I always wanted to be on my feet but, initially, wasn't allowed on them. The muscles in my legs just weren't strong enough to carry my body weight. I hated this fact. At nine-months-old I didn't understand why. All I knew was that I wanted to be up, but I was stopped in my tracks. As you can imagine, this caused more than a few tears.

There was some good news though. I had a baby bouncer which I enjoyed going in, even if it was adjusted so my feet only lightly touched the floor.

I had to wait until I was about 18-months-old, when I was allowed to put weight on my legs. To do this I had to wear orthopaedic boots called Piedro boots.

No pretty, little shoes for me. I know that sounds awful. They were made of soft, white leather but not what a little girl would want to wear. I had to have boots because they gave my rather weak ankles support.

So, equipped with my boots came some hard work. Not necessarily for me, because walking and being on my feet was what I wanted to do, like most 18-month-old babies, but it was hard work for my parents.

Unable to walk or stand on my own, whoever was walking me had to hold me from behind on the hips. This must have been back breaking. By working with me in this way they had proper control of my body and could adjust my feet to make sure they were flat on the floor.

All the time my whole body was getting stronger. Eventually I could sit up on my own. However, there were many occasions when I fell over with someone having to help me sit up again. This was just the way it was.

I was determined these setbacks were not going to stop me. Although still being held at this stage, I was getting better at walking every day.

I also had to get used to the splints on my legs. These were called ankle/foot orthosis or AFOs and they helped to control any abnormal movement on the foot or ankle during walking. I had to be measured for them and recall having a plaster cast on each leg from which the measurements for the AFOs or splints were taken. The splints came up to just below the knees and were fitted into my Piedro boots. The whole purpose of wearing splints was to give support, especially to my ankles, and to keep my feet straight and flat on the floor.

I had to wear splints for many years. Sometimes I wore boots with them and sometimes specially fitted trainers, neither of which were very girly or pretty.

I didn't like having to wear Piedro boots or splints. Both were firm and, after a while, wearing them could be very uncomfortable, especially in hot weather. The splints were made of plastic and had a lining of thin foam. There was a velcro strap at the top of the splint and another across the ankle.

Although I could choose the colour of the boots, it didn't alter the fact these were 'special' boots I 'had' to wear. Eventually, Piedro brought out some trainer boots which were marginally better. They were still heavy looking, but at least the white trainer boots did look more the part.

Then, at last, a breakthrough! I was allowed some 'normal' trainers to wear at home. These still had to be chosen carefully, having to be wide enough to fit the splint in and still giving me the support, but they were a definite improvement.

There were times when I would go to parties. On these occasions, I would have loved to have worn pretty, girly shoes, but there was no way the splints would fit in them.

I always felt 'different' as my friends had pretty, party shoes and then there was me. Yes, I always had a pretty dress, but I could never have the nice shoes I wanted to finish off the outfit.

Then there were the many questions. My friends and peers would ask about my splints and boots, wanting to know why I was wearing them and children I didn't know would often stare and point. Having people stare and point is something I have had to grow up with. I believe this is down to lack of education and this is something that today, I am trying to address.

I wore my splints until the age of nine, but continued to wear the Piedro trainers until my mid-teens.

There were many types of shoes I was unable to wear as a child and this situation is no different today. Winter shoe shopping is easier than summer. I am a big fan of long boots so, as long as they don't have a high heel, then any boot is pretty much suitable for me to wear.

With summer shoes, it's a different story. My shoes should have a certain amount of support and whilst I do wear some slip-on shoes, they must fit well so my foot doesn't slip in and out. I can wear a very slight heel, but heels of a significant size are a definite no-no, as are any shoes with either low or no backs.

Nowadays, I go mad over my winter shoe shopping and buying my nice long boots. It must be a country-girl thing. During the summer, you will see me in either trainers or a particular brand of slip-ons.

Emma Sheardown

Anyway, back to my early years.

Liz, my physio, also played an important part in my physical development, largely thanks to getting me walking with a rollator. The first two rollators I had were ones I pushed. I still needed someone with me and, like any toddler learning to walk, there were many falls.

It is amazing to think that though I fell over many times, other than a few cuts and bruises, I never seriously hurt myself. As I look back over my 34 years in amazement, it's incredible to think that after all the falls I have had, the only thing that I have ever broken are my two front teeth! But more of that later.

In those early days, If I fell, somebody would pick me up, dust me down and off I would go again. I wanted to be like my able-bodied cousins and friends so much that nothing would put me off.

As I grew out of my second rollator, the next one was called a K-walker which went around the back of me so I pulled it along as I walked. Eventually I got to the stage where I didn't need any support from anyone unless I fell over.

Another problem for me in those early years was walking on my toes. I was always being told to keep my feet flat. Mum and Dad would frequently remind me by saying "heel, toe", "heel, toe". This is something I still have a problem with today and get 'reminded' about. Even now I think about how I am walking. It is particularly noticeable when I am tired. Wearing the splints certainly helped in the beginning.

I would hate to count how many pairs of shoes I have worn out at the toes. Probably hundreds! The irony is that the remainder of the shoe is usually in quite good condition. It's just because of the way that I drag my toes.

As I drag my right foot even more than the left, it has been known for the left shoe to be in near perfect condition, whilst the right shoe is ruined.

When I am shoe shopping, I tend to shop for practicality with the toe being the most important thing to consider. I try, where possible, to buy shoes with a sturdy looking toe as, without this, I know the shoe won't last two minutes. Is that something you think about when shopping for footwear? I'm betting not.

When I am out, I often look at nice, modern, high-heeled shoes and can only imagine what it must feel like to wear them. I often joke that I would probably break my ankle. The truth is, I wouldn't get that far, as I wouldn't even be able to stand up, let alone have time to fall down.

Both my grandfathers helped with my walking in their own way. On a Sunday, if they were with us for lunch, they would have two broom handles at the ready.

With Grandad Sheardown at one end and Grandad Harry at the other I would walk holding onto the poles from one Grandad to the other. They used the bribe of a one pound coin to encourage me to walk, and that usually did the trick.

It was on one of my regular visits to see physio, Liz, that my life was to take on an exciting new turn. The world of horses and horse riding was to open up for me at the tender age of two.

Speaking to Mum, Liz suggested riding would be ideal to help with my physical development. It would help strengthen my core and help with balance and co-ordination.

Mum and Dad talked about it but hadn't completely made up their minds. But then, a couple of days later, something amazing happened. My occupational therapist called to say she had got a Shetland pony I could have. It was fortunate we lived on the family farm and this made the decision easier.

Dusty Bin arrived the next day. She was a brown pony, quite scruffy looking and dusty, hence her name. Aged about 24, she wasn't very tall, about nine or 10 hands, but what she lacked in stature she made up for in attitude. Shetland ponies are known for their feisty temperament and Dusty was no different.

Like all horses and ponies, Dusty needed regular grooming. I wasn't old enough or even physically able to groom her but I would sit in my pushchair and watch whilst someone else groomed her.

I would ride her whenever someone was free to take me but, of course, I always needed to have two people with me - one to hold and lead her and one to lift me on and off and support me, either by holding one of my legs or supporting my back.

I loved riding Dusty, right from my first ride, and I was always excited to go out on her. I always loved going around the field with her. However, like a lot of Shetland ponies, Dusty was a bit of a character, a bit naughty at times - especially when she had a nibble of either Mum or Dad.

This was the start of my love of horses but, more importantly, at that stage of my life, using riding as an extension of my physio was the best thing to help me.

Having Dusty Bin was far from plain sailing and there have been more than a few stories of her exploits shared over the years.

One day I wanted to go across the field to see Dusty so my Auntie Chris walked me. Suddenly, out of the blue, Dusty came cantering up behind us and kicked out. I remember Auntie Chris picking me up and flinging me out of the way. This meant my poor aunt got the full force of Dusty's kick, right on her shin bone! Fortunately, there were no broken bones, although I think Auntie Chris was rather sore for a few weeks, and I have never been allowed to forget it!

Although Dad loved his animals on the farm - his dogs, cattle and sheep - he knew nothing about horses. Mum's interest and knowledge of horses was even less. However, to their credit, they took on the challenge.

To make things even more complicated, Dusty had an obvious dislike of men, which meant it was left to poor Mum to do everything with her.

However, I remember one day it was decided I didn't need Mum to walk next to me and that Dad would lead me around the field on his own.

Well, that was alright until Dusty decided to buck and I fell off and landed on my head, narrowly missing the water trough.

Getting bucked off was very scary. Being so young I didn't understand what was happening. One minute we were walking along quite nicely and the next it was like Dusty exploded. Her hind legs went up and I was catapulted through the air.

Luckily I had a riding hat on as I literally landed on my head. Mum and Dad took me to Grantham Hospital to be checked over, but no damage done.

Falling off Dusty-Bin didn't put me off riding one little bit and I was soon eager to get back on, with Mum by my side.

All was well until in June 1990 the unthinkable happened.

One morning we woke up and looked out of the bedroom window to find Dusty Bin laid on her side in the field. Sadly, she had died. To say I was very, very upset is an understatement. I loved that pony so much.

After Dusty died I didn't ride for a little while. I was devastated. On a practical note, Mum and Dad knew riding was helping my physical development so they wanted to find somewhere for me to ride so I would continue my therapy.

They tried two local riding schools. One was closing and the other didn't take children under seven. This one was a Riding for the Disabled Association or RDA centre, so I waited until I was seven and signed up.

During the time between losing Dusty and joining the RDA, an RDA group near Lincoln would take three ponies to school and we took it in turns to ride them. I think this happened once every two weeks, depending on the weather, which was great.

Going to a Christmas craft fair at Barkston Village Hall, in November 1993 my love of horses was reignited again. I had already started riding with the local RDA Group, Kesteven RDA by then.

Whilst at a stall I bought a book called 'Bomber The Pony Who Thought He Was An Aeroplane'. On the next stall was a lady whose daughter went to Brownies with me. Quite out of the blue she said "I've got a pony that might suit you". Mum and Dad arranged to go and see the pony the following weekend and, very soon after, we went and collected her.

The pony was a 14.hh Palomino called Pal. Having Pal meant I could ride on the farm again with the help and support of Mum and Dad.

I had Pal for about two years. Unfortunately, after my dad had an accident and injured his ankle, he was no longer able to look after Pal, so reluctantly she had to go back to her owner. Once again, I had lost a pony. I remember being so upset when Pal went back and begging Mum and Dad to let me keep her. Sadly, it wasn't to be.

Physically, by the age of six, I could walk 'on my own', but always had somebody walking behind to catch me if I lost my balance.

Until one day that all changed. I remember like it was yesterday.

I was sitting in one of the easy chairs in our farmhouse living room. It was late afternoon, heading towards tea time and Mum was in the kitchen getting food ready. I think Dad was still out working on the farm.

I remember sitting there thinking 'I want to walk' and nobody is around to help me. 'I'm going to walk' so that's what I did!

I stood up out of the chair, got myself balanced and then I set off. I took two or three steps before very proudly announcing "look Mummy, I can walk!!". I was so, so excited I could finally walk like everybody else and, from that day on, nothing and nobody was going to stop me.

Mum remembers the events of that day, as I do. She also remembers, after my 'announcement', putting her head around the kitchen door to see me stood there with a great big smile on my face.

We were both so excited, neither of us could wait for Dad to get home from work to tell him the good news and show him.

From then on there was no stopping me. On a week's holiday to the Algarve in Portugal a few days later, it wasn't much of a holiday for Mum and Dad as I wanted to walk everywhere. Long hotel corridors were great for perfecting my 'solo' walking skills, as they were carpeted (which gave a soft landing) with loads of space. Mum and Dad were reluctant to let me walk in our room because the floor was tiled and were worried in case I fell and hurt myself.

We had a lovely holiday. The weather was hot and, in between all the walking, I loved sunbathing by the pool.

Speech

About this time I started regular speech therapy. It is difficult to describe what my speech was like. I could say different words and put words into small sentences but they were distorted so it made it difficult for people to understand what I was saying. I suppose it's like most babies when they are just beginning to talk. Parents do eventually begin to understand what they are saying and I would imagine mine were no different.

My first speech therapy sessions involved the speech therapist making different sounds and encouraging me to do the same. These exercises were repeated at home. I gradually worked towards saying every day words like 'Mummy', 'Daddy', 'please' and 'thank you', although I might have said 'ta' instead of thank you. Like everything else, I had my homework to do.

My speech has improved so much over the years but I still worry people can't always understand what I am saying or switch off when I start to talk. If I am tired my speech can sound slightly slurred.

In recent years I have faced discrimination twice whilst on the telephone. One call was with my bank, HSBC. I was asked if I had got a cold because the advisor I was talking to said she couldn't understand what I was saying. I explained I had a slight speech impediment but she insisted she didn't understand me. Fortunately, Mum took over the call.

On the second occasion, I had several phone calls with Vodafone, my mobile provider, regarding my contract renewal. During the first two I had hardly said two words when I was either accidentally cut off or they put the phone down on me. On the third occasion, I got the opportunity to say a bit more but the caller said she didn't understand me and ended the call.

Mum was so disgusted she phoned straight back and complained. Guess what? I never heard another word from them so I cancelled my contract.

However, following on from my experience with Vodafone, I was pleased to have the opportunity of working with them. As part of the disability awareness work I am now doing alongside my motivational speaking, I provided training aimed at those staff who handle calls from disabled customers or clients.

Instances like this seriously knock my confidence when I'm speaking on the telephone. Mum assures me I speak quite clearly and encourages me to make my own calls. I am not always comfortable talking to people I don't know but now, when I make a call to someone new, I start by explaining I have a slight speech impediment and, if they don't understand me, encourage them to tell me so I can repeat my message.

Interacting With Other Children

As a baby, Mum took me to the village mother and toddler group once a week and, when old enough, I went with my cousin, Rachel, to play-school in another local village. My Auntie Christine used to go as my one-to-one to give Mum a break. This was great as it gave me the opportunity to interact with able bodied children, which was very important. I am grateful to my parents for letting me do these things.

Aged five I joined the local Rainbow group, Barkston Rainbows, and, once again, could interact with my able-bodied peers.

I used to go to Rainbows on my K-walker and loved mixing with the other girls.

I would wear my Rainbow tabard which, for our pack, was red. The tabard fitted over my clothes and had a pocket at the front that I used to put my subs in. Once I had said my Rainbow promise at my enrolment, I was given my triangular enrolment badge which Mum sewed on the front of my tabard. I remember feeling quite proud of myself in my little uniform with my badge.

I followed on from Rainbows by joining 1st Barkston Brownies, aged seven. I loved having the opportunity to mix with children from the village and by the time I started Brownies, I already knew a lot of the girls from Rainbows.

My Brownie uniform was very different to that of my Rainbow tabard. We had the choice between a khaki brown pair of jogging bottoms or a khaki brown skirt. I hated wearing skirts and therefore chose the joggers. Both our polo shirts and jumpers were yellow and had the Brownie logo on. Our 'accessories' included a yellow neckerchief with a brown woggle, a yellow peak cap, a khaki brown sash to put our badges on and a brown belt with a purse on it.

I always felt proud wearing my uniform as it made me feel like I belonged to something. That 'something' had nothing to do with disability and everything to do with my overall development.

I remember that my 'six' was Pixies and eventually I became a Sixer, which I was very proud about! For the uninitiated, Brownies are split into small groups called Sixes with the Brownie in charge of the six, called a Sixer. She has the responsibility of making sure everyone in the group can take part in activities and that their voice is heard.

I always loved doing the work to achieve my badges and, by the time I finished Brownies, aged 11, I had a sash full of badges I had earned. My badges represented a range of activities and teachings, from cookery and art to road safety and crime prevention… and lots more in between.

There were one or two badges I was unable to do. The 'walking badge' - I remember asking Mum how far four miles was… well, that was never going to happen, was it?

It was whilst I was at Brownies that I had the first taste of being in the big wide world on my own. Brown Owl and her helpers were brilliant. They would help me and encourage me to do things, but they would also let me get on with it and didn't treat me any differently to the others.

I never received any type of discrimination or unkindness during my time as a Rainbow, Brownie or Guide. However, I do remember two girls at Brownies so intent on helping me that they wouldn't leave me alone. They would literally grab my arm as soon as they saw me. Their caring nature was lovely, but a little over-baring. I remember getting upset because I didn't want to be rude or ungrateful, but I longed for my independence and to be treated like all the others. In the end, my mum spoke to Brown Owl about the situation and she spoke to the girls without upsetting them.

At various points throughout my life I have experienced this sort of behaviour with people taking over or over helping. It is a very difficult situation, but over the years I have learned to be more confident in talking to people about it.

One thing I cover today in my disability awareness talks is the importance of people 'offering' their help as opposed to just assuming and jumping in. If somebody tries to 'take over' and help me without asking, I always politely say "thank you very much, but I am ok" or ask them to help in a different way.

Having thoroughly enjoyed my time at Brownies I was keen, when the time came, to move onto Guides. At that time Barkston didn't have a Guide pack so I went into Grantham and joined 2nd Grantham Guides.

There were a couple of girls who moved onto Guides as well, but there were a lot of new faces for me to get to know. In some ways joining Guides was a tougher transition. I suppose that as I got older, although I was much more stable on my feet and independent, in some ways, the gap between what friends were doing and what I was able to do, widened.

So, although I was always determined to find a way around things, there were things that, with the best will in the world, just weren't physically possible or safe for me to do. I found these situations frustrating. I just wanted to have a go and, somehow, the things I couldn't join in with seemed so much more fun.

I did enjoy my time in Guides and, as with Brownies, I progressed and earned various badges. After nine years in guiding, I decided to leave Guides when it came to focusing on my GCSEs.

These activities were all part of my development and interacting socially with my peer groups in my early years. A very important stepping stone for what was to come.

CHAPTER 3

LEGACY, LAMBING AND LIFE ON THE FARM

I was lucky enough to be brought up on the family farm. My family has rented the farm from the Thorold family since 1931, shortly after my grandad and nana were married.

The farm has been in the hands of three generations of the Sheardown family. My grandad, Harold, ran the farm until my dad took over after leaving the local agricultural college in the nearby village of Caythorpe.

I have got three half-brothers from Dad's first marriage. Martin and Phillip followed in Dad's footsteps by studying agriculture. Like Dad, Martin studied at Caythorpe whilst Phil went to Riseholme. Also like Dad, on their graduation from college, they both joined their dad on the farm.

Unlike Martin and Phillip, my half-brother, Andrew, didn't pursue a career in farming, instead he went into banking and eventually set up his own business.

The farm was run under two businesses - HW Sheardown and Son, after my grandad, Harold Wallace and JT Sheardown and Son, after Dad, John Thornton.

Dad had a partnership in both farms, he and Martin had a partnership in HW Sheardown and he also had a partnership with Phillip in JT Sheardown.

Both Martin and Phil still work the farm today, having taken over from Dad when he retired in 2007.

Over the years, even I have seen big changes on the farm. Back in the day, the farm was both arable and had sheep and cattle, with Grandad and Dad enjoying their cattle and sheep. Martin and Phil, on the other hand, were more interested in the arable side - I think, really, they just like playing on their tractors!

Over the years leading up to Dad's retirement, gradually the farm changed. First of all, it was decided the cattle would be sold as looking after them took a lot of time and effort, especially in the winter when they were housed in the barns. Dad had reached the point where he was struggling to manage them and Martin and Phil weren't interested in taking them on. It was a few years later, for the same reasons, the decision was made to sell the sheep.

This was a sad time. I loved the farm and, most importantly, I loved spending time with my dad there. Dad had a great love of animals and I have inherited that love because I have always had animals in my life.

We always had a flock of breeding sheep and a herd of beef cattle. From an early age, I would go with Dad in the Land Rover to check on the sheep. Whatever the weather, winter or summer, I liked nothing better than going with him around the farm.

Lambing time was an especially happy time for me, I loved it! Before I could walk with my rollator, Mum used to take me in my buggy and we would go around the lambing pens. Then I got to the stage where I could walk with my rollator around them.

Doing this was quite a challenge. The pens were always set up in the Dutch barn. There were always eight to 10 pens either side of the barn with a walkway down the middle. Whilst there was plenty of room for me to walk down, the ground was uneven and so I used to get my wheels caught on stones or down holes.

Mum or Dad were never too far away in case I fell or got stuck. I often used to fall over in the yard or in the barn, but I was fortunate that I never seriously hurt myself. I often got cuts and bruises on my hands, elbows and knees though. Mum or Dad would pick me up and comfort me as I would be upset and sore. After they cleaned me up and had made sure I hadn't seriously hurt myself, I was always ready to get back on my feet and back to the lambs.

With time my navigating skills improved. I learned to navigate my way out of trouble and became more aware of where I could and couldn't go.

To watch a lamb being born was exciting and special. This new life taking its first breath and watching Dad make sure its airway was clear was beautiful. Dad would lay the newborn at the side of its mother and I would watch the ewe clean the lamb. It was amazing. Invariably the ewe would have a second lamb or even a third one and the whole procedure would be repeated. We would leave her to it and then go back later and check that all was well.

A lot of ewes would be able to lamb on their own and many did, especially during the day if they were in the field. They were always kept in a field near the farm where my dad or one of my brothers would keep an eye on them. Some of the sheep would need help, especially if they were carrying a big lamb or if it was twins or triplets.

At night, they were brought into the lambing shed so it was easier to keep an eye and protect them from the weather. They were long days for my dad and brothers and lambing lasted for about six weeks. It was an extremely happy time for me, but extremely tiring for them.

As I got older, I was allowed little jobs around the lambing pens, but can you imagine the scene? Me wobbly, jerky, holding onto my walking frame and trying to put a ladle of food into the trough in the pen and this big woolly sheep trying to get the food out of the ladle. It was certainly entertaining. Some of the food would land in the trough but most would end up on the floor or even in the wool of the ewe.

Giving them water was also an interesting experience. Something else that if entirely left to me would have resulted in them going thirsty. Despite this, I was always determined to have a go. I loved being allowed to try.

I remember on one occasion I was trying to fill a water bucket up to take to one of the ewes in the pens. I went to the water trough and, as I stretched over to fill up the bucket, I let go. As I leant over the water trough to reach for the bucket, I fell in… head first! I was absolutely soaked and I remember Mum taking me home and putting me straight in the bath to get me cleaned up and warm.

When we got home, I followed Mum into the house and stood at the door sobbing "I'm wet and you don't care!"

I am sure my brothers thought I was a nuisance but if they did they never said anything… well, not to me anyway.

My biggest thrill was when Dad allowed me to lamb a ewe. With his help, of course, but wow, how excited was I? To start with, I needed help to kneel down, then Dad had to keep the ewe still.

I am not squeamish at all, which was certainly a good thing given what I had to do. In fact, I was very eager to stick my hand up inside the ewe and feel the lamb. I remember being worried about pulling out something that I shouldn't!

I need not have worried as everything was quite self-explanatory. Of course, as everything was warm and slippery, one of my biggest challenges was trying to get a grip on the lamb. I couldn't get a firm hold of its legs and so Dad had to help me.

When the lamb was delivered, Dad showed me how to clear the airways. I always loved putting my finger in the lamb's mouth and letting them suck on it.

We then placed the lamb by the ewe's head so she could lick her new arrival.

I feel very lucky to have had the chance to experience this. What a thrill it was to have helped bring new life into the world.

Lambing time was always a happy family time where we all got involved. We always had cade or orphaned lambs. Sometimes the ewe had rejected the lamb or she had a multiple birth and couldn't look after them all. This was usually if they had had triplets and Dad would take the weakest one away from the ewe. That meant the cade lambs would need regular feeds with a bottle. If I was feeding one, Mum would sit me on a bale of straw and place the lamb on my knee, supporting the lamb while I fed it. My cousins, Louise, Steff, Rae and Andy also loved to come to the farm and help around the sheep.

My dad also enjoyed showing cattle at the Christmas Livestock Markets at Grantham, Newark and Melton Mowbray. He and my grandad showed for many years and won many trophies. There were four trophies they won outright. This meant they won one category for three years in a row.

After Dad died, Martin, Phil, Andrew and I took custody of one trophy each. My trophy will always be very special to me as it is a legacy from Dad and Grandad. I now keep my trophy in a safe place, although I often get it out as I love to read all the inscriptions. I feel so proud to be a custodian of such a special memory of Dad, Grandad and the family farm.

Before I started school, Mum would take me to the shows to watch my dad showing. He also enjoyed judging cattle and was often invited to judge at shows in Lincolnshire, Derbyshire and Staffordshire. Mum and I enjoyed going with him.

My cousins, who regularly spent time at the farm with me, played a big part in my life. They never saw me as being any different. Yes, they knew I had a disability but it didn't make any difference to them. They played with me, carried me around and did my exercises with me.

Rae is 11 months older than me so we were close and still are. As small children, we not only played together, we went to mother and baby swimming and play group.

In the school holidays, we would have a day with Rae's grandma, Gran Diggins. She would take us for walks around the lakes and feed the ducks, or go and see the horses. Then we would go back to Gran's and make cakes. They were happy days.

On reflection, it's no surprise my early years surrounded by a family who shared my love for animals was to positively shape my future. The signs were already there. I just had to connect the dots.

CHAPTER 4

TAKING TO THE SADDLE

Where it all began: riding around the family farm on Dusty Bin, aged three.

Little did my parents know, that Liz's suggestion of riding would turn into a lifetime of passion and achievements.

At five years old, I had started St Francis School. Once a week St Francis were visited by ponies from the Park Riding for the Disabled Association (RDA) group. This enabled me to continue with riding, which was great! The sessions were run by our physios and took place in the school playground. We did various exercises with the physios whilst sat on the horses.

One exercise was called 'Around The World'. This wasn't a favourite exercise of mine as we had to spin around on the horse - taking one leg over the horse's neck to sit sideways and then continue around the horse until returning to sit the correct way facing forwards.

One year a group of us took part in an RDA fancy dress competition at Newark County Show. Our theme was Robin Hood and I was Little John.

By the age of seven, I was mad keen on horses and riding. The riding school in the nearby village of Hough-on-the-Hill also ran a riding for the disabled group, Kesteven RDA and, much to my delight, by this age I was old enough to go.

To begin I had half hour private lessons with the owner and instructor and her helpers. The first pony I rode was a black mare called Lady. I used to ride once a week with my therapy riding gradually incorporating skills needed to learn to ride.

During this time, I went on to ride other ponies. Sunny, was a grey pony who I remember being quite fast - in fact it was Sunny I experienced my first 'accidental' canter on. Splash was another grey pony and the complete opposite to Sunny. Being quite a slow pony, he was the absolute perfect pony and a real favourite. I also progressed from riding with somebody leading me to being 'let loose', then riding off the lead rein and eventually progressing to trotting.

It felt amazing to be making so much progress. Being let loose off the lead rein gave me a sense of freedom and a real sense of achievement. To think my instructor thought I would be able to 'control' (steer, start and stop) my pony made me feel like I really could achieve. To get to this stage, I had to learn to make Lady walk on, make her stop and steer her. Being able to do these things brought about extra challenges for me. A very different experience than that of an able-bodied rider.

For those of you unfamiliar with horse riding let me try and explain what I mean.

Being able to ride requires core strength, being able to control and 'quietly' use my limbs as well as fine motor control - all these are an extra challenge for someone with quadriplegic cerebral palsy.

Firstly, I needed to work on and develop my core strength as this would enable me to sit up tall, straight and in balance with the pony. My instructor would do exercises with me whilst I was sitting on the pony that would help to develop and strengthen my core stability and balance. These exercises would include stretching an arm out to the side, in front of me or above my head.

To begin with I would do this with one arm at a time and then progress to both arms together. These exercises were to challenge my core, as in doing them with my arms it meant I would have to rely on my core stability for balance and be less reliant on my arms for support.

Next came my tight, unruly legs. At this stage in my riding, I would require my legs to remain long down by the horse's side and have a loose, but supportive contact there. My heels needed to be down and my ankles loose. This requirement was a far cry away from my tight, curled up legs.

When I got on the pony, my mum or dad would massage my legs and give them a stretch as an attempt to loosen them off. This need for me to stretch has always been the case. Even later, during my competitive career, my trainer would often have to stretch my hips and legs out for me to be able to tune into my horse. I also had a stretch routine I would do prior to getting on my horse every time I rode, both to train or compete.

My arms, as with my legs, would need to be still and under control, but not rigid. I would need them to be loose and required my shoulder, elbow, wrist and finger joints to be soft and supple - again, totally opposite to my 'normal' way of being. In the early stages of my riding I suppose my arms weren't quite as important as I would hold a handle on the front of the saddle, rather than holding the reins. However, as my riding progressed, my whole body became looser and both my arms and legs became less tight.

During the latter years, my warm-up stretch routine would also include stretching and loosening my arms.

You can probably see by now how riding fitted in nicely with my physiotherapy program - and believe me, physio on ponies was much more fun than laying on the floor doing boring stretches.

Over the years, my core strength, as well as the coordination and control of my arms and legs, have significantly improved and I am now a hundred times stronger and more co-ordinated when I am riding than I was. However, even now the same can't be said for my head, which still wobbles all over the place.

As I learned to ride, through my teenage years and competitive years, riding was and still is a great physio. The emphasis might have changed, in that my goal now is to do exercises to improve my skills to become a better rider. However, in doing these exercises to make me a better rider, I am also still helping my body.

Since 2012 and training full time with Angela Weiss, we stripped everything back and took me right back to basics which, at that time, was exactly what needed to happen.

During this time, I learned so much about my body. I have had to work very hard with my off-horse exercises to become the rider I want to be. Instead of physiotherapy, my off-horse work has included both gym and biomechanics work.

Biomechanics is based on the study of how skeletal and muscular systems work under different conditions. My biomechanics work would be adapted, according to areas I may have been struggling with on the horse. For example, if Angela said to me I was slipping in the saddle, then I would tell my biomechanics coach and he would give me some specific exercises to help strengthen that area. I also found the bio-mechanics work not only helped my development as a rider, but was also good for my CP.

I suppose you could say that as my level of riding and training has gone up, so has my physical ability and control over my body and, in turn, this has had a positive impact on my general physical health.

Back in my teenage years, whilst still riding with the RDA, there were times when I began to feel frustrated. I always started my lesson on the lead rein and could never quite understand why? In my head, I didn't need to be on the lead rein anymore and I always saw this as a backwards step.

To add insult to injury, when my cousin Rachel started riding it didn't seem long before she was learning to canter and jump ... and there I was still on the lead rein most of the time. Whilst I loved that Rachel was riding too, this highlighted the difference in our ability.

Looking back, seeing Rachel being able to progress in a way I 'couldn't', made me even more determined! I think I was always realistic though and realised there would be limitations. Therefore, I re-focused myself on the goal of developing my trot work. By now I was able to trot off the leading rein, but there was still lots to work on and improve on in the trot work. This re-focused me on a goal that would develop my riding further and would be a challenge, but at the same time was more realistic.

Becoming a Brownie also helped me move deeper into the world of horses and horse riding. Whilst I was at Brownies, I met Frances Smith. Frances and her mum, Gill, had horses and Frances and I soon became good friends. During the school holidays, we would go to each other's houses to play. I, of course, loved going to Fran's house as we spent time with the horses. At that stage Fran had a pony called Cavalier and Gill a horse called Prince.

I used to have a ride on Cavalier. During my first visit Gill tried to get me onto Prince, but he was just so big.

Gill and Fran also taught me about looking after the horses and, as the best way to learn is to do, they used to let me help around the place. I'd muck out, groom and feed the horses. I would also ask lots of questions and learned a lot.

Fran used to compete regularly at a local show and gymkhana held in Londonthorpe village. Eventually she got a new pony and Charlie and I would be entered in the Best Turned Out class, which I loved. I was so grateful to Gill and Fran for giving me the opportunity. They would regularly take me with them to shows, I just loved being there with them, watching Fran and just being part of it. Of course, I was also learning too.

It was during my time riding with Kesteven RDA that I had my first taste of competition in the form of RDA Handy Pony competitions. These were obstacle courses where you were required to weave in and out of cones, move hoops from one post to another, trot over a pole, etc. I loved having the opportunity to do this. It was great to have a go at a new challenge.

I also enjoyed going on two holidays with the RDA. We went to the Clwyd Special Riding Centre in Wrexham, Wales. Set in the welsh countryside, it was an amazing place. The centre offered residential riding holidays to groups. They had a beautiful bungalow style accommodation block where each bedroom was named after a famous horse. There was a communal room where we ate and my mum came along too as one of the cooks.

Riding at Clwyd was incredible. Not only did they have a large indoor arena to ride in, but they had specially designed tracks. These tracks weaved their way around all of the centre's fields. What made them so special was that they were surfaced with pieces of rubber and fenced, making it a safe place to ride. There was even a picnic area half way around which had a space for horses to rest and have a drink whilst we enjoyed our picnic and a specially made water area that could be made deeper or shallower for us to ride through.

Thanks to the high levels of safety put into place on the tracks, I could enjoy my first hack, or ride out. Out of the arena and into the countryside, we were off the lead rein with my instructor riding too. This gave me an incredible feeling and a real sense of freedom. The only time that I had experienced anything close to this before was when I had been on the lead rein whilst riding on the country lanes at home. But my riding experience on Clwyd's special tracks was something extra special. Here I had the best of all worlds. In a countryside setting, a safe environment with fences around me and a soft, rubber surface. My instructor also rode a horse, so it was just like going on a 'normal' hack - it felt great! These holidays were so amazing.

I continued to progress with my riding but, as I got into my mid-teens, I became increasingly frustrated at the reality of the things that I was physically unable to do.

Being told I couldn't do things with the horses never went down very well. I always considered myself sensible. I knew my limitations and I knew exactly what was safe for me to have a go at and what wasn't.

However, there were times throughout the years, when I felt my own intuition was ignored. Some people would think I was silly for wanting to try to do certain things when I was keen to stretch that comfort zone, push boundaries and move forward positively.

This is no different today and I would never put myself in danger if in any doubt.

Then reactions like this would knock my confidence straight down. So much so, that I would almost give up, and stand back - anything for a quiet life! Today no more!

It wasn't just the cantering and jumping, but the fact I couldn't lead the horses, tack them up or groom them that bugged me. I so wanted to be involved in looking after them. Things had to change and I was determined that they would. This was when a new chapter of my life began as I started to compete in RDA dressage.

CHAPTER 5

SCHOOLS, BRAS AND ANIMAL MAGIC

I made Princess Diana laugh when I showed her my computer work and had referred to the Prince of Wales as Prince 'Chiles'. Pic courtesy of Lincolnshire Echo.

A t the tender age of four, the time came for my parents to think about what school I should go to.

Initially the first thought was I would attend the local village school. Attending a mainstream school would have meant having a one-to-one assistant to help me get around and cope with school life.

During this time Mum and Dad had been told about St Francis Special School in Lincoln. St Francis catered for children aged 2 to 19 and who had a range of disabilities and medical conditions.

On visiting St Francis Mum and Dad were impressed with what they saw. They had all of what you would look for from an educational point of view, but with the added benefit of having all the therapists I required on a daily or weekly basis, on site. This meant I could continue my important therapy programmes and follow a full-time education programme.

Mum and Dad took comfort from the attitude and reassurance from the headteacher. They explained the most important thing at that stage in my life was to get me onto my feet and walking and that I had my whole life for education.

I eventually started St Francis in 1989. I travelled an hour to and from school every day by taxi. I remember it took me a good few weeks to settle and I used to take comfort in driving the red and yellow toy car in the play area.

My first teacher was Mrs Kay and we also had two classroom assistants, Mrs Coulson and Mrs Jagger who helped with classroom work, continuing therapy as well as generally looking after us.

My weekly therapy programmes included a continuation of physiotherapy sessions, speech therapy and occupational therapy. Alongside which I also had a hydrotherapy session every week with the physios in the school's hydrotherapy pool. These sessions also included 'dressing and undressing' where the physios would help us learn how to dress, undress and dry ourselves.

Being able to carry out these everyday tasks has always been a challenge.

Over the years it has got easier, partly down to my own development and partly because I have learned how to adapt, I have learned what helps to make life easier and I know what type of clothes are easier for me to wear.

When it comes to showering, I have always found drying myself with a bath towel difficult. This is due to co-ordination as well as being able to put enough pressure on my skin to get it dry. I have always struggled to dry my back as I have difficulty in wrapping the towel behind me.

Nowadays I use a towelling robe which I put on as soon as I get out of the shower. This means the robe dries my back and shoulders (the difficult bits) whilst I dry everywhere else.

When drying I always sit down and prefer to sit on the bed as it gives me stability, room to move and adjust myself without falling.

Even sat down dressing has its challenges, particularly when picking my legs up to put trousers, pants and socks on, it is easy to lose my balance. You will have noticed I refer to trousers. I am not a 'girly girl', I never, ever wear skirts and only on very special occasions will I wear a dress.

I struggle with buttons and zips, so wherever possible I buy either trousers with elasticated waists which, let's face it, within the realms of fashion, are few and far between, or trousers that have hook and eye fastenings.

However, I said that I can adapt and I do. Sometimes Mum will sew a hook and eye on trousers that have buttons, whilst on trousers that have a bit of 'give' in them, I don't undo the buttons and just pull them over my waist.

As for bras, well they are a nightmare! If wearing a conventional bra, I put it on backwards, behind my back so the fastening is at the front. It is then pot luck as to how long it takes me to co-ordinate the eye over the hook and then I turn the bra around. I usually wear sports bras that I can pull over my head. Even they have their own challenges, especially in the hot weather as they stick to my skin and roll up.

The process of showering, drying and dressing myself usually takes me the best part of an hour. I never like rushing around, mainly because if I try and 'speed up' I end up being slower as my hands and fingers won't work as quickly as I want them to. I always allow myself plenty of time to get myself sorted. At least two hours from getting up to leaving the house.

When it came to eating and drinking at this stage of school, I used to have lunch in the physio department. This was so the physios and occupational therapists could help me learn how to use a knife and fork and try out various special plates, cups and pieces of cutlery to make drinking and feeding easier.

Eating and drinking and being able to use a cup tied in with my portage work. At this stage my arms were very jerky, but I had more control over my right arm than the left. I have worked hard over the years to strengthen my left hand, but it is still the right arm/hand doing most of the work. I am famous for my 'I'm a little teapot' stance. This is because my left arm is weaker and naturally wants to curl up, as explained earlier.

When it came to learning to eat, I had a wooden handle which looked a lot like a plunger. It was stuck to the table with a rubber sucker, for me to hold onto and keep my left arm under control. I also had a 'jelly mat', more correctly known as a Dycem Mat, which was like a non-slip rubber matting. The 'jelly mat' was put underneath my dish or plate to stop it slipping.

Firstly, I learned to eat with a spoon and eventually progressed to a fork. With my poor fine motor skills, there is not enough on a 'normal' spoon or fork for me to grip so I started out with a thick foam handle which was slipped onto the spoon or the fork, making them easier to hold. I then moved onto a fork and spoon with a plastic yellow handle. Again, this gave me more grip than that of a 'normal' fork, whilst being a step up from the fork with the foam handle.

I was never able to use a knife due to the poor control in my left arm/hand, and I still can't. From the fork with the plastic handle, I moved onto a splade - a fork that also had a blade on the side. Being right-handed, the blade was on the left-hand side of the fork. I still use one of these today and find it so useful being able to have both pieces of cutlery in one hand.

There are certain foods, such as meat and vegetables, I am unable to cut up. In order to hold and cut, you need both hands with a knife and a fork. When eating out I ask somebody to cut my food up for me. I find it very embarrassing. There are also occasions when I have to ask for something to be changed to make it easier for me to eat. An example would be an ice-cream sundae. As they are served in a tall glass with a long spoon, I can't reach in and bring the spoon back out without the ice-cream going everywhere! Having to ask if my sundae can be put in a bowl is not as embarrassing as it would be if I got my ice cream everywhere and made a mess.

When I am out, I don't take my splade with me and sometimes I will try and cut my own food up with a knife and fork. In these situations, I put my fork in my left hand and try to keep the food still. Then I use the knife in my right hand to cut - sometimes it works and sometimes it doesn't!

As for drinking, I use a straw. This is because of my jerky movements and involuntary reactions. I have used a straw ever since I became too old for beakers with a lid and a spout. A good move to ensure everybody around me stays dry.

It's also my jerky movements that stop me being able to pick a drink up, as obviously as soon as one of my muscles jerk, then the drink goes all over.

Lucky for me a lot of people use straws nowadays … although, I do get a few funny looks when using a straw to drink a glass of wine!

At school, the classroom assistants played an important role in continuing my physio work throughout the rest of my school day. They would be there to walk with me whilst I got used to new walking frames, when I progressed to using tripods or when I had new splints to get used to. They would also help me develop my co-ordination and fine motor skills whilst doing classroom activities.

In the classroom, I had different pieces of equipment to help me with sitting at the desk as well as with writing and computer work.

To be able to write or colour, I had the same set up as I used to eat.

I had the wooden bar to control my left arm and the Dycem or 'jelly mat' to stop my paper from slipping whilst I was writing or colouring. I still rely on my 'jelly mat' today when I am writing, I couldn't be without it. Initially I had a foam handle around my pencils so I could hold them more easily and eventually these were replaced with a rubber, triangular grip. The grip was to get me to hold the pencil properly, by using the three sides of the triangle to place my fingers and thumb on. As with many things, I have never got to grips with the correct way of holding a pen and have developed my own unique style.

I had a kneeling stool to sit on, both at the classroom desk and the computer. The kneeling stool encouraged me to sit upright and helped develop my core stability. A kneeler put me in a position that was correct, stable and supportive, allowing me to concentrate on whatever I was doing. I always liked sitting on my kneeler, as I felt tall and in a good position to be able to do things with my hands.

The first kneeling stool I had, had side blocks on both the seat and the knee stool so I didn't wobble off. The classroom assistants would have to help me onto the stool. I would get onto it and then they would put the blocks on, to make sure I was secure and in a correct position. I also had a block which went between my knees to give me good posture and stop my knees drawing together.

Computers have played a vital role throughout my life, as although my writing has improved loads, I soon get tired arms and, in this case, get slower, with my writing becoming less and less legible. I literally couldn't manage without a computer. Whilst at school, I relied on the computer for all written work. Without one it would have taken weeks to write an essay and the teacher would have been unable to read it!

My first computer was a BBC Master, a far cry from today's technology. You could write, save and print on it and play a couple of games. The word processing program was called 'Stylus' - I can see it now, a black screen with a red curser and white text. If I remember rightly, there was only one font and one font size. There was something exciting about using the BBC Master, though looking back now it was very boring.

On my BBC Master, I had a special keyboard - at least twice the size of a normal keyboard - with a key guard over it. The keys were bigger and in their own little 'hole' so it was easy for me to 'hit' the key I wanted.

I then progressed onto an Acorn computer. With this I had a key guard over a 'normal', standard keyboard. By this point technology had advanced to computers having 'mice'. Instead I had a tracker-ball, which I found much easier to use.

Over the years, improvements in technology have really helped me. Predictive and suggested text on Apple products reduces the time in which it takes for me to type, which is always a big help. I have tried various pieces of voice recognition software, however there are none that will respond to my speech.

Today, I still spend a lot of time on my PC or iPad developing my brand and my work as a motivational speaker. As well as sending emails and keeping my social media up to date, I also do a lot of my planning, marketing and developing presentations using my PC. I couldn't be without it.

During my early days in the classroom, I progressed through school as anyone else would, all the time developing physically and educationally. By the time I was six and in class two, I was walking 'on my own' - everybody, my parents, family, therapists and staff in school had all worked so hard with me and, by this point, it was paying off.

It was during my time in class two when I met HRH the Princess of Wales for the second time. March 1992 and both the Prince and Princess of Wales were visiting different organisations around Lincoln at the time.

Princess Diana visited our school. I was very lucky that day as I got to meet her twice - our first meeting when I was chosen to present the princess with some flowers on her arrival. On that day, I did wear a dress, a little floral one. As a special 'treat' I wore a pair of 'normal' black patent shoes too.

Weeks before I remember being told I had to curtsey. You can imagine me learning to curtsey, can't you? By that point I had only been walking on my own for about nine months. But, I was determined I was going to do it.

By the time the day came, with the help of Mum and Dad, I could do my own version of a curtsey. I was a bit nervous, but I also felt very lucky I had been chosen to do it.

After the presentation, the princess had a tour around school. She came into my classroom (class 2). I was on my BBC Master computer and she knelt at the side of me. I must have been writing about the Prince and Princess of Wales, as I wrote something about Prince Charles. The Princess laughed as I wrote the Prince's name and then pronounced it as Prince 'Chiles'! It's a lovely memory.

As the years went by, my therapy programmes decreased as the need for my speech therapy and occupational therapy programmes stopped. I continued my physiotherapy programme, though further down the line and, into my teenage years, I discharged myself from this service. I felt my physiotherapy sessions didn't benefit me and I had reached the point where it was now down to me to continue working my own physical development. The exercises I was doing during my physiotherapy sessions had served their purpose.

During my schooling years I followed the national curriculum in the same way my able-bodied peers were doing, but being at a special school gave me time to learn and develop at my own pace. I also had teachers and classroom assistants on hand to give me any extra support required.

At the age of 10, there was another important decision to be made about my education - whether to continue through to secondary at St Francis or make the change into a mainstream secondary school.

We visited several schools in Grantham. I came out of the first school crying. I was over-awed at the sheer scale of the school, the stairs, the long corridors between classrooms. After visiting all the schools, it was decided I would stay at St Francis.

From an educational point of view I am sure this was the right decision. I spent my secondary school years in a small class, with the majority being peers and friends who I had been with throughout my school life.

When it came to GCSEs, because our school was small, we only took a handful of them.

By this point, when it came to thinking about the future, I had set my heart on a career in the animal world. I decided I wanted to go to the University of Lincoln's Riseholme College Campus to study for a National Diploma in Animal Management - that was my focus. I knew I needed A to C grades in maths, English and science to be accepted onto the course.

Unfortunately, at this stage, we didn't do GCSE science at our school, so this did cause some concern. However, I was told for the time being I should focus on my maths and English. I wasn't particularly a fan of English. I hated reading - so much so that when our English teacher went around the class asking what books we had read, while my friend Katie would reel off a great long list of books, I'd slump down in my seat and cautiously admit to reading none. I was so, so bad, but I just couldn't get into reading. From my point of view, there was nothing worse. I even tried to convince everyone I couldn't see properly, but unfortunately for me my eyes were given a clean bill of health by the optician. I was very disappointed!

I think the English teacher almost gave up with me in the end. I suppose she could see she wasn't going to win and soon twigged it was a waste of her breath to keep asking. If I was forced to read a book, I would simply ask someone to read it to me. Times change eh? Now look at me!

Despite my disability, I have always been active, so I found sitting still reading to be a boring pastime. I would much rather be 'doing' something else. Nowadays, I will read autobiographical books of people who I look up to. I love learning about their lives and how they came to be following the career or path they are on. Whilst I might inspire or motivate people in what I am now doing, I also like to be inspired and motivated myself.

With maths, I had a love-hate relationship. I enjoyed it, but I wasn't very good at it. Fortunately, my teacher, Mrs Smith, was great. Lovely, kind and funny and, because I so, so wanted to achieve and improve in my maths, she would always be there to give me extra help and support. My dad was also good at maths, so he too would spend time helping me. I think that Mrs Smith and Dad deserved a medal by the time they had finished with me.

I 'hated' algebra with a passion and could never work out why someone had the bright idea of combining letters and numbers - why?

I received my GCSE grades in the summer of 2001. I ended up with a D in maths and an E in English. This wasn't good enough and certainly not good enough to be accepted into Riseholme.

Fortunately, I had another two years left at St Frances until I was 18, giving me time to quickly re-focus, my goal now to make the most of those two years and work so hard I would achieve those important grades.

I had already decided prior to receiving my grades I was going to stay on at school in Post 16. Post 16 focused more on the independence side of things and preparing us for the future. I was a little concerned about going into it as I was more interested, at this stage, in achieving those grades rather than the activities on offer. I was determined to make the most of it though.

I shouldn't have worried. School re-organised Post 16 to make sure my peer group could continue our academic education.

I committed myself to round two of GCSE maths and English, focusing on achieving those C grades. My teachers also arranged for me to go to Yarborough high school, next door to our school, to do my GCSE science course.

This was great, I had a new opportunity to focus on the subjects I needed for college.

My mind was set on studying Animal Management. Animals, horses and the farm were all I was interested in. I loved all animals and seemed to have a special connection with them. At this stage, I wanted a career that revolved around looking after and caring for them. At the time, I would have done anything to achieve my dream of going to Riseholme and pursuing an animal related career. I remember thinking, what's another two years?

For those two years I committed to working hard. I would work during break times and after school on a Monday and Wednesday, I would go over to Yarborough school for science and, on a Tuesday, would stay behind for extra maths with Mrs Smith.

I didn't let myself off in school holidays either and would go home armed with textbooks so I could continue striving for those C grades. Mrs Smith used to love me when I would return to school after the school holidays with a pile of work for her to mark.

During this time I also studied English literature which was quite a challenge for someone who didn't usually pick up books.

Finally, in the summer of 2003, all my hard work paid off. I finished school with my important C grades in maths and English, in science I got a D and, amazingly, I got a B for English literature!

On receiving the grades I had a mixture of feelings. I felt incredibly proud of myself, for literally putting everything into achieving those grades and earning my place at Riseholme. But, at the same time, I felt relieved that those two extra years at school and everybody's help and support had paid off.

Having been at St Francis for 14 years, I was really sad to leave. I was also extremely grateful for what everyone had done in helping me achieve, both physically and academically. It had been an incredible time for my self-development.

Now I was more than ready for the next chapter.

CHAPTER 6

MARY, UNI, HELLO PARA DRESSAGE

B eing brought up on the farm gave me a real insight and love for the animal world. It was clear from quite an early age that any career I chose would involve animals.

Mary Branker CBE was a friend of the family. She was well in her 80s and a retired veterinary surgeon. She had a wealth of experience within the veterinary field. Mary's career included being the veterinary surgeon for Twycross Zoo, chief veterinary surgeon for the Department of Environment, Food, Fisheries and Rural Affairs during the 1960s foot and mouth outbreak and carrying out animal welfare inspections on behalf of government officials. She was the most extraordinary lady. I would sit listening to her amazing stories all day long. She had so many tales to tell and the most witty sense of humour.

So, when it came to mulling over career options in my head, Mary was the perfect person to talk to. I was well-aware I would have to be realistic when it came to what career I would physically be able to pursue.

Mary didn't want to answer me straight away, instead she went away to give it some serious thought. I couldn't wait until I saw her again to find out what she had come up with. Mary suggested I could look at animal behaviour or something in the research field. I liked the sound of animal behaviour so I went for it.

In September 2003, I enrolled at the University of Lincoln's Riseholme campus on the national diploma in animal management course. This was a full-time, two-year course. However, it was decided I would do the course part-time, three days a week, over three years.

I couldn't wait to get to Riseholme and start my animal career.

My first weeks at Riseholme were a bit of a shock. My time there had its ups and downs as I struggled to adapt to my new environment. I enjoyed my course, but I struggled to adapt to college life - so much so that I would look forward to my days off so I could focus on my assignments in my own environment.

The campus wasn't huge, but to me it seemed enormous. The animal care unit, the kennels and the cattery were at one end of the campus whilst the library and most of the classrooms were at the other end.

Due to its sheer scale it was decided I would use my mobility scooter to get around. This was okay for getting between buildings, however when it came to getting into the classrooms in Riseholme Hall, which was an older building, there was a problem. With steps to get into the building and no handrails I had to rely on other people to 'give me an arm' and help me to get in. I hated having to do this and, if I was on my own, then I was stuck. It wasn't until I was well into year two that handrails were finally put up, making life much easier.

I struggled with making friends at college. I felt like a small fish in a very big pond. I had gone from being in the safe, 'protected' environment of St Francis, with friends that I had been with since the age of four and support staff to help and support me, to being completely on my own, or at least that's how it felt. This was very scary and, with the access difficulty, I felt so alone and totally out of my depth.

There were times when I felt like quitting but, fortunately, each time I thought about giving up, these thoughts were followed by the realisation I couldn't give up. I had worked so hard to get to Riseholme and I knew if I quitted, I would deeply regret not achieving what I set out to do.

Another frustration was when lectures only lasted half the time they were supposed to or when lecturers 'forgot' to turn up.

As part of my course, I was required to do work experience. I was lucky to get a place at our local veterinary centre, Avenue Veterinary Centre in Grantham. I went to Avenue vets every Friday morning throughout my three-year course and thoroughly enjoyed it.

It was great being there once a week as I got to know the vets and the nurses well. I did a lot of observing as a lot of the tasks carried out by the nurses, I wasn't able to do. These hands of mine just weren't delicate enough. However, there were plenty of other jobs for me to tackle, such as cleaning the operating theatres and preparing the sterile surgical kits. I learned all about the different equipment in the kits. My job was to make sure each kit was complete with all the tools, drapes and swabs and then sealed to ensure it remained clean and sterile. I also helped where I could with any bathing and grooming and, of course, I was always on hand to provide cuddles for the animals in our care.

During time there, I also watched many operations, mainly on dogs and cats. I saw many spay operations and castrations. I was especially interested watching one of the partners, Richard Huddart, perform ortho-paedic operations on dogs. For surgery, I had to wear a green operating smock - not very fetching, but hugely important for protecting the patient from any infection getting into the operated joint. I was never squeamish and found these operations extremely interesting. I used to watch in awe at the vets' knowledge and their ability to navigate their way around the complexity of an animal's innards. It all looked very complicated to me but, nevertheless, I learned an awful lot from the experience.

Looking back now, I am so, so thankful that I persevered and completed my course. I know that if I had let my fears and uncertainties dictate and had given up, I know one-hundred percent that I would have regretted it.

I often wish I had my time at Riseholme again, although I know you shouldn't look back with regret. I know that the Emma of 2020 would totally embrace college life with confidence and enjoy every minute.

In the summer of 2006, I graduated from Riseholme with a dis-tinction grade in my national diploma. I was thrilled and surprised. I didn't expect that at all. I couldn't work out how I had managed to achieve top grades when I battled a negative feeling about college and felt like I had struggled. Having said that, I did work hard when it came to my assignment work and projects.

I was also proud and rather surprised when I was presented with the trophy for the most improved student during the 2005/2006 year. Again, how could somebody who struggled so much with being there be crowned 'most improved student of the year'? I don't know, maybe it was for that simple reason why I won.

My distinction grade also meant I had earned enough UCAS points to move onto a degree course. I did apply to go onto the BSc Equine Science course. I had wanted to do the BSc Equine Sports Science course, as I felt this would give me a good background at a time when I was just embarking on my Para Dressage career. However, as this course at Riseholme involved a lot of riding, which I wouldn't be able to do, there was no way around for me to be able to do it. Instead I focused on doing the Equine Science course.

In the end, as my Para Dressage career was taking off, after a lot of thought, I decided to put my degree on hold. Having the opportunity to pursue a career in Para Dressage was a dream come true and a once in a lifetime opportunity.

Nobody could take my animal management qualification or my UCAS points away from me and I decided I could do a degree anytime.

Para Dressage was providing me with an amazing opportunity to really make something of my riding. I just 'had' to take it and I have never, ever regretted that decision.

CHAPTER 7

FAIRY AND THE
SYSTON FLOCK

Emma Had A Little Lamb

Her Fleece Was White As Snow

And Everywhere that Emma Went

That Lamb Was Sure To Go

August 1995. I had been told by Mum and Dad that in six weeks' time I was getting a surprise. Wow! I couldn't wait and spent the next six weeks in anticipation, trying to guess what it could possibly be.

Eventually, after what seemed like a long time, Sunday 25th September arrived. A friend of my grandad and Nana Sheardown, Doris Bellamy came for lunch. After lunch, Mum, Dad, Auntie Doris and I got into the car ready to drive to my surprise.

October 1999 and the big smile says it all, with ram lamb, Syston Whiteboy.

When we got to Belton village, Dad made an excuse to call at Michael and Julie Coney's at Belton Grange. Belton Grange is the home of the Belton Flock of Lincoln Longwool sheep.

Dad told me to get out of the car and there was my surprise - a Lincoln Longwool ewe with a pink ribbon around her neck! She was called Belton Fair Maid V (quickly shortened to Fairy) and was a gift from Auntie Doris and my dad. I was so excited to have my own sheep and was eager to learn all about her. We went home and Dad and I picked the trailer up so we could bring Fairy home.

Belton Fair Maid V (Fairy) was eight months old, being born on New Year's Day. She was the fifth down her blood line to be called Fair Maid - hence her name Fair Maid V, her mother was Fair Maid II.

Dad fenced a section of the field next to our house so I could keep Fairy there. She had a couple of Mum's Jacob Sheep in the field with her for company.

I always went out with Dad to feed Fairy and the Jacobs at night when I got home from school and at weekends. I would very often have to let Dad put the feed into the trough, as all the ewes were bothered about was their food and not whether they knocked me over.

One year on, Autumn 1996, I decided I wanted Fairy to have a lamb and now was the right time to put her to the ram. So, Michael Coney kindly let me borrow Belton Kingswood … and five months later, on the 7th March 1997, Fairy had a ram lamb. In the January, for my twelfth birthday, Michael and Julie made me a member of the Lincoln Longwool Sheep Breeders Association and registered my flock. From that day I had my own flock (well, a flock containing one sheep). My flock was registered The Syston Flock, flock number L874.

Why the Syston Flock? Syston was one of our local villages and part of our farm came under the parish of Syston. The farm that my Grandad, Dad and now my brothers farm is called Syston Grange. The landlord of our farm was the Thorold family who lived in Syston. The Thorold family once owned the number '2' flock of Lincoln Longwool sheep. My flock, many years later, took on the prefix 'Syston' with the flock registration number 874.

When Fairy had her lamb in the March, this was to be the first lamb of my new flock and named with the prefix 'Syston'. The Lincoln Long-wool Sheep Breeders Association have a system for registering lambs each year, whereby each year all lambs born are named beginning with a letter. 1997, the registration letter was 'T'. I therefore named my new ram lamb "Syston Tom".

The next thing I wanted to do with my sheep was to show them. Because Tom was born late in March I had to wait until Heckington show in July to show him. Tom was in a big class of 14, the majority being two months older than him, having been born in January. Considering the age gap it was great that he finished in seventh place.

Heckington show also held the annual Lincoln Longwool Sheep Breeders Association sale. I was keen to expand my flock and so went home with the third edition to the flock, Hutch Starlight (Star).

That year I had two ewes to go to the ram, Fairy and Star. On the 18th January 1998, Fairy gave birth to another ram lamb, Syston Unicorn. When Unicorn was born, he was a good, solid ram lamb. He was a big lamb with very good confirmation. Confirmation is "the desirable and undesirable skeletal and muscular structure of an animal." In other words, he was a super example of his breed.

Lincoln Longwools may not have long legs but as a "large volume sheep" have "substance of bone to carry their weight."

To put it bluntly, Unicorn was a fabulous example of his breed who ticked all the boxes. At this stage, I just didn't realise what a superstar he was destined to be.

During the show season of 1998, I showed Unicorn in the ram lamb class. I was thrilled when he started winning classes and fellow breeders complemented me on what a good ram lamb he was. By the 1999 show season, Unicorn had grown into what Dad and I thought was a good example of a Lincoln Longwool ram - he was now a shearling ram (one year old).

My flock was now rapidly growing. During the 1999 lambing season, I had five ewes lamb and seven lambs born. 1999 was a year I will never forget. So many exciting things happened right from the beginning.

This year the registration letter for lambs born was 'W'. Lambing started even earlier with my first lamb born on the 2nd January. It was Fairy that lambed and this time she gave birth to a ewe lamb, Syston Winifred Mary. Winifred Mary was named after two very special people in my life.

My Nan B's name was Winifred Mary, so when I discovered the names of lambs born in 1999 were to begin with 'W', I promised my Nan I would name one after her.

As mentioned in Chapter 6, we were friends with a retired veterinary surgeon, an amazing lady also called Winifred Mary so it seemed like a lovely tribute. Both Nan B and Mary were delighted to have a lamb named after them.

Four days after Winifred's arrival, another of my ewes, Tara was due to lamb. I got home from school that night only to discover Dad had taken her to the vets where she had undergone a caesarean section. Fortunately, both Tara and her ewe lamb survived. Apparently before the vet had stitched Tara up, her lamb was wandering around the surgery, hence the nurses giving her the name, Wanda.

The next ewe to give birth was Star with twin ewe lambs, Whizz and Whitney. Unfortunately, Star was unable to look after both, so Dad decided it would be better to leave the stronger lamb, Whitney with her mother and bring Whizz, who was struggling, into the house. We had Whizz living with us in our living room for the first week.

Dad brought in a wooden crate with straw for Whizz to lay in and we put her in front of the Rayburn to keep her warm. We used boxes, fireguards and magazine racks to keep her in. I absolutely loved having her in the house. It wasn't that different from caring for any other baby.

When Dad first brought her in, she was so weak he had to feed her by a tube which went down her oesophagus so the food would quickly get into her stomach. He got enough milk for the first few feeds by milking Star because, like with any baby, the first milk is always important as it gives the lamb vital colostrum. By giving Whizz a couple of feeds using her mother's milk, she made it through and was soon able to feed from a bottle. We had to feed her every four hours and, of course, clean her wooden crate out at regular intervals.

When she got bigger I would take her into the garden where she would follow us around skipping and jumping. I was like Mary and her little lamb. Being brought up by us meant she saw us humans as her family. I absolutely loved this time with her as she got to know us and relied on us. I loved holding her and giving her cuddles. We would play on the lawn and then she would follow Dad as he worked on his vegetable garden.

Of course, there was a serious side to all of this, in that bringing her into the house saved her life. For me, I had a unique opportunity to build a special bond with this little lamb. For a lot of people, sheep are just big wooly things that all look the same and spend their lives following each other, but when you get to know them individually, as I did, you soon realise that, like any animal, they all have their own individual characters.

My love of sheep runs deep. I always loved spending as much time as possible with them. If Mum and Dad lost me, I would be out in the field with them. I soon discovered I could coax them into trusting me with none other than digestive biscuits.

The whole flock had a taste for digestives, even Fairy, who wouldn't come anywhere near me, but would succumb for a biscuit. This was very special.

Unicorn also loved digestives, but when we were at a show, his favourite treat was ice cream. I am not a big ice cream fan, so Unicorn would quite happily finish my 99 for me. He wouldn't get a look in with the chocolate flake though!

During the 1999 season, I showed at six shows including 'the BIG one' - my first Lincolnshire County Show. My show team were Unicorn in the shearling (one year old) clipped ram class and Winifred Mary and Wanda in the ewe lamb class.

I was thrilled when Unicorn won his shearling ram class. I hadn't expected I would be successful with it being THE county show for the county breed. The Lincolnshire show is the event all competitors wait for and those who have bigger flocks often save their best stock for this one.

Winifred Mary and Wanda came 2nd and 5th respectively in their class.

The next stage for Unicorn, having won his class, was to go into the male championship class, where he was up against the winners of the class for two shear (two years old) and the ram lamb class. Usually the two shear rams win the male championship largely because they are shown in full wool and therefore are a clear representation of the breed so I 'knew' that Unicorn wouldn't win. How wrong could I be? To my absolute amazement the judge walked over to Dad, Unicorn and I and declared that Unicorn was the male champion!

Being male champion meant we then went onto the class for overall or supreme champion - the final class of the show between the champion male and the champion female. Again, the ewe that we were up against was a ewe in full wool so going with the tradition of the breed I expected her to win. Yet again I was in for a big surprise as Unicorn was crowned supreme champion.

Wow! This was amazing, I was so surprised. I couldn't have imagined winning the county show, but we had!

To add to Unicorn's success in the show ring, I also entered Unicorn's fleece in the fleece competition. This had been clipped off him in February. The competition was judged by the British Wool Marketing Board. Unicorn's fleece also won the championship for medium luster wool. It was an incredible trio of wins.

Just to put the icing on the cake, whilst taking part in the grand parade, Unicorn, Dad and I were introduced to HRH Princess Anne. It was a little bit nerve-racking. As the princess said 'hello' to Unicorn, I prayed he didn't head-butt her. The princess asked Dad and I about Lincoln Longwools and wanted to know about Unicorn. Meeting the royal visitor on that day was a special way to end an amazing week.

I went on to have another successful lambing and show season in 2000. Although Unicorn wasn't as successful as a two-shear ram in the show ring, he now had lambs of his own running around in the field.

2001, I remember well. However, it wasn't for the same, positive reason as in 1999.

Grantham livestock market. 22nd February. Three words dominated the conversation. Foot and Mouth.

As a youngster growing up on the farm, during the school holidays I used to love going to the market on a Thursday. Apart from the business side of it, which I had mixed emotions about, the market was always a social event for local farmers. Dad would enjoy his weekly catch up with his farming friends and there was always a bacon sandwich involved somewhere.

It was the half term holidays. All the farmers were talking about a disease called Foot and Mouth which had been found on a farm in England the day before. I remember listening carefully to what Dad and his friends were saying, but at this stage I didn't understand at all the severity of the situation and the huge impact it was to have on British farming.

As Dad and I travelled home in the Land Rover, I started to ask questions as I was keen to learn what was going on. It was obviously important to Dad and his friends. When we got home, the headlines on the lunchtime news were dedicated to the 'foot and mouth crisis'. Every single day the situation got worse and worse. Every morning the first thing Dad, Mum and I would do was to switch the news on so we could check how the disease was spreading. It was spreading further and further around the country with more and more cases being confirmed.

I wanted to watch the news - after all farming was who I was - and I wanted to know what was happening. But the TV was full of heartbreaking images, either of animals being destroyed and their bodies being cremated in pyres, or interviews with farming families who had lost their animals and their livelihoods. I was so scared our farm would be affected. The thought of losing our animals, including my own sheep, was petrifying.

Like with every farm, Dad and my brothers, Martin and Phillip, put barriers and disinfectant pads in place to protect our animals. For us, this wasn't an easy task. Our farm was quite open and, in the middle of the site, were other businesses, such as a pig farm, a mushroom farm and a plant hire - all of which relied on traffic coming through. This meant Dad, Martin and Phil were limited in how much protection they could give. The farm had three entrances. Two were blocked off, leaving one entrance/exit that everyone had to use. At that entrance Dad and my brothers made a disinfectant pad, laid a bed of straw across the farm entrance and dowsed it with disinfectant. This meant the wheels of every vehicle were disinfected

The disinfectant pad had to be replaced regularly. With so many vehicles using it, it would soon get churned up and need changing. I was the first to moan at Dad when this happened. It was such a stressful time and I wanted to make sure we were doing everything we could to keep our animals safe.

The threat of Foot and Mouth also meant we were unable to transport animals anywhere. In turn it meant no shows.

Eventually the transportation ban was eased a little and we could start to move animals again, but there were a lot of regulations to follow.

In the September, I wanted to transport a ram I had sold to his new home. This was quite a process. First I had to apply for a movement licence, then Dad and I had to take the empty trailer to Bourne, 12 miles away, to be sealed by DEFRA (Department for Environment, Food and Rural Affairs) officials. Sealing the trailer meant the DEFRA official would wash the trailer out and disinfect it, then they would put seals on all of the doors. The seals were like metal fastenings which could only be undone with proper cutters used by the DEFRA official.

The same official would then visit the day after to check my paperwork and escort us whilst we transported the ram to his new home. Dad and I would then have to go back to Bourne to start the disinfection process again.

Thankfully, at the end of 2001 into 2002, Foot and Mouth began to die out. For those of us fortunate to have escaped the disease things began to return to normal. I was so grateful we had survived and things were improving. However, it was hard to forget how many animals had lost their lives and how many human lives had been devastated too.

We started showing again in 2002 and I showed for another three seasons. By this point the Syston Flock had grown to over 20 sheep.

One day, as my flock was growing, Dad said I had to sell some. I hated selling them, especially when we sent them to market. That was a real ordeal. I knew deep down, unfortunately, this was part of the job. I will never forget the day I said to Dad "I'm just going to see Unicorn", to which he replied "Oh… you can't, I have taken him to market". As you can imagine, I was furious and very, VERY upset.

I loved my sheep. I would spend ages in the field watching them and talking to them. It was important to me to be able to do as much as possible with the sheep on my own. Dad would spend time fencing off smaller pens in the field that I eventually took over to make all my sheep safely accessible to me.

Unicorn always had his own special pen. I think both Dad and I always had a soft spot for Uni. Having said that, weighing in at 19 stone at 18 months old, Uni often used to head butt Dad where, in contrast, he was as quiet as a lamb with me.

I used to spoil the sheep with their favourite treats of digestive biscuits and Uni's 99 at a show.

We carried on showing until the end of the 2004 season, but then a change in personal circumstances meant we had to make some difficult decisions.

Sadly, Dad was struggling with arthritis. I had to rely on Dad to do all the manual work with my flock as there were things I just couldn't physically do. So, with Dad's arthritis developing, we knew we had to sell the flock.

However, I was very lucky when Michael and Julie Coney decided to buy my whole flock. I couldn't have been happier. My flock were returning to their routes and were only down the road which meant I could go and see them. Michael and Julie also agreed to keep Fairy for me. Fairy lived out a happy life and died at the place where she was born, aged 12.

My years of caring for and growing the flock had taught me so much… by having my own flock and because Dad made everything accessible for me, it gave me a real insight into caring for animals - great grounding for my future career.

CHAPTER 8
DAD

Dad and I outside Grandad and Nanna Sheardown's at Syston Grange.

M y dad, John Thornton Sheardown, was the nicest, kindest man you could ever meet. Dad was a gentleman. I don't think I ever saw him get flustered or even get cross.

Dad and I were the best of friends and I loved nothing more than spending time with him out on the farm and in the countryside. He taught me all about the farm. I loved to learn about the cattle and sheep, although I wanted to learn about all aspects of the farm, the crops and machinery as well. Dad always let me have a go in terms of looking after the animals. He would go out of his way to make the sheds and fields accessible for me so I could help.

With my own flock of Lincolns, I wanted to be able to access them all easily and safely so I could look after them on my own as much as possible. I had my flock in the six-acre field nearest to our house. Dad fenced off half the field for me with the other half still being used for the farm's flock.

As my flock grew, so came the need for more separate field space to house the rams, the weaned ewe lambs and the weaned ram lambs. This meant sectioning different parts of the field off and building large pens or small paddocks to house the different members of my flock.

The thing I always appreciated was that if I came up with a suggestion of where and why I wanted a new pen built, after a couple of days of thinking about it, the trailer with all the fencing equipment would come out and, with my supervision, of course, my new pen would be built. Dad also put additional gates up so I could get around all the sheep without going in with them and getting knocked over. Eventually, as Syston Unicorn grew into a big, strong ram, Dad and my brothers built me three permanent pens or small paddocks. One of the pens gave Unicorn a safe place to graze, that even he would not be able to head butt his way out of.

During lambing time, Dad and I would go around the farm in the Land Rover shepherding. We would feed the ewes and, when they had finished eating, we would tip the feed troughs over to stop them getting wet if it rained. We would go around the fields to check the ewes and lambs were safe and well and, if we encountered any problems, Dad would teach me about them and I would help where I could.

I had been going out with Dad and Mum around the farm since I was just a few months old. Mum also enjoyed having a ride around the farm as it got her out of the house. She liked to see what was going on and would always be on hand to give Dad help when needed.

It wasn't until I was about two years old and able to sit up on my own that Dad would put me in my car seat and take me around the farm on his own. When it got to the stage where I was walking with my rolator, this would come with us too. This meant I could get out of the Land Rover at various points around the farm. I especially liked being on my feet whilst Dad tended to the cattle or sheep.

I loved my Dad so much and I think that's where I got my love of animals from. Mum would always say he would talk to the animals in a more loving way than he did to her… not at all because he didn't show his love to mum, but because he was often to be heard calling a ewe or a cow 'darling'. I think that's partly why I loved being with him so much. It didn't matter whether you were his daughter, his wife, a friend, someone he barely knew or an animal, he would always do whatever he could to help you.

I think he was pleased I took on his love of animals. As said before, my two brothers were more interested in the arable side of the farm, while the cattle and sheep were important to Dad and my grandad, I guess Dad could probably see, somehow, I would follow in their footsteps.

Dad and I worked well together. I was always asking questions and wanting to learn from him. We would often share a laugh and a joke whilst we worked. Dad was the biggest wind-up merchant ever and I am lucky I have inherited his sense of humour.

I am always, always grateful for the childhood I had. Being brought up on the farm gave me great opportunities. I do believe the animals on the farm, alongside Dad's help and encouragement to get involved, was influential in my physical development.

Other than the love of animals that we shared, I think I am also lucky to have Dad's strong work ethic. He always liked to get things done and if he saw a job that needed doing, he would do it, otherwise it would 'niggle' at him, which is just like me.

When it comes to personality traits, I see both Mum and Dad in parts of my personality. I would love to say I have got my dad's placid temperament, but there are occasions where I can be more fiery.

I am also like Dad when it comes to time management. Whilst I enjoy a lie-in on a day off, if I am on the yard or have an appointment, then my alarm is always set, giving me plenty of time to get ready and either prepare or get to where I need to be. Just like Dad, I hate to be late and have the same attitude - it is better to be half an hour early, than five minutes late.

I often laugh when I am waiting for Mum, I will always say "I am always waiting for you, I spend half my life waiting for you!" - this is something my dad always used to say to me.

I learned so much on the farm. I learned very quickly about life and death. Dad used to say the thing that sheep could do better than anything else was die. It sounds awful, but it's true. Particularly when the ewes were in lamb. It was so easy for them to lay down and become over-thrown. This meant they could not get back up and if nobody was around to help them, sadly, they would die.

Whenever a ewe or a lamb died, I always felt upset for the one left behind - whether it was a ewe grieving for the loss of her baby or a lamb bleating for its mother.

I can't remember the first time I experienced a sheep dying, but I know that both my dad and grandad talked to me about this from an early age. Another saying of theirs was "where you have got livestock, you will also have dead stock". This saying might sound harsh and to the point, but sadly it is the reality.

Whenever an animal on the farm was sick, Dad would always do his very best for them, but sometimes his efforts just were not good enough. Dealing with the loss of an animal doesn't get any easier. I think a loss always hit Dad hard and I am certainly no different. I also learnt a lot from Dad about nature and wildlife. Whilst we travelled around the farm, he would point out different animals and birds to me.

Our farm had been a base for American airmen during World War II and was full of relics, including an intact underground shelter. Dad was a little boy during the war and would often share some of his experiences with me. He could remember hiding under the stairs during air raids as well as bombs being dropped in certain fields. The field next to Syston Grange, where my grandparents lived, was used by the American servicemen for games and PE, especially baseball where, I believe, they had two or three pitches.

In 1993, the 50th anniversary of when the Americans came to Barkston Heath, Grantham Museum put together an exhibition. It focused on the stories of the American servicemen based in Grantham. The museum contacted Dad regarding their time at Barkston Heath. They wanted to know if Dad could remember Carl Garmus. Carl was stationed at Barkston Heath and he, along with others, used to spend evenings at Syston Grange with my grandparents. In fact, Carl and my nana used to arrange parties at Syston school for the local children. I understand the Americans could always get any amount of fruit and sweets, or candies, as they called them.

When Grantham Museum got in touch, Dad was still in contact with Carl, along with some of the other servicemen. Arrangements were made for Carl to come over from America for the celebrations and he stayed with us for five days.

What a lovely man. He was about 83 when he visited and was flown over on British Airways who sponsored his return flight.

I have always been interested in history, particularly the world wars, and living on our farm was like living in a World War II museum. I used to love exploring the relics dotted at various points around the farm. One day when I was studying World War II at school, Dad cleared the underground air raid shelter on site to make sure it was safe, then took me down to explore. It was an amazing experience. The shelter was like a tunnel. On the top was grass and earth, which disguised the fact the shelter was there, and the inside structure was built from concrete.

I was about eight when Carl came over from America. I loved learning about his time at Barkston Heath as he reminisced with Dad.

I also loved learning about my sheep. I feel extremely lucky to have shared my time with The Syston Flock with Dad. Although the flock was mine, I always thought of it as ours. Dad had a great love of farm stock. Dad and my grandad showed beef cattle successfully for years and won four trophies, including the Grantham Challenge Cup at the Grantham Fatstock Show. After we lost dad in 2012, my three brothers and I took custody of one trophy each.

Dad and I had a great partnership in developing The Syston Flock. Dad would help and support me and teach me everything I needed to know about being a shepherdess. He taught me about the day-to-day care of the sheep - about feeding, worming, trimming feet, keeping their bottoms clean, shearing, worms and parasites – all the important husbandry for keeping my flock healthy and thriving. Of course, for obvious reasons, a lot of these things were left to Dad to do, although it was always important to me that I learnt about what he was doing and why and how he was doing it.

Dad also taught me about the paperwork and procedures, which, unfortunately, became a big part of keeping sheep following various health scares discovered within the sheep and farming world.

We thoroughly enjoyed our time showing as a family, enjoying the social side of being part of the Lincoln Longwool Sheep Breeders Association too.

Dad also played a big part in my early horse riding. He took me to my lessons and helped during them.

He was on the committee for Kesteven RDA and would always be the first to offer to do things for the group, even if it meant my brother, Phillip, getting his welding tools out to make something.

Dad was also my biggest critic. It had been known for him to set cones out in the yard so I could practice my 10 metre circles on my tricycle. When I started competing, Mum would video all my dressage tests and Dad would sit with me and watch them. He didn't know anything about dressage, but would soon tell me if my halt wasn't square or if my 10 metre circles were more like 15 metre hexagons.

Mum supported me too, of course, but was always a bit apprehensive, especially when my 'mounts' got bigger.

I was 18 when things changed. In 2003, whilst on holiday in Cornwall, Dad's hands suddenly became swollen. All the joints in his hands became inflamed, so much so he was unable to drive for the rest of our break. We didn't know it then but this was the beginning of arthritis which, sadly, developed into a serious lung condition.

Gradually Dad's breathing began to deteriorate too. At the beginning, his illness was put down to 'Farmers Lung', a condition seen in farmers milling animal feed, harvesting, dealing with hay and straw and breathing in the dust, without any protection. Today, this would be a health and safety issue and, whilst carrying out such work, protective masks would be worn with better ventilation.

In 2003, Dad was referred to a lung specialist. It was soon revealed that his lung condition, fibrosis of the lung, was linked to his arthritis.

As his breathing deteriorated further he used an oxygen machine at home. Forced to significantly cut down his work on the farm, in true determined Dad style, he would go out on the land in his truck, just to keep his eye on things.

Watching Dad's health deteriorate was heartbreaking. Seeing someone you love - your Dad - regularly struggling to breathe and do the things he had always done...I can't put into words what that was like.

To begin with, Dad tried to continue with daily activities, such as fetching the milk and papers from the village, taking my greyhound, Rosie for a run around the field and taking me riding. He would still do odd jobs around the farm. However, in between times, he would spend time on his oxygen machine.

Eventually Dad had to rely on his oxygen more and more and was no longer able to work on the farm at all. It was horrible to see him stuck in the house and barely able to move away from his oxygen machine. It just wasn't him. He was meant to be out on that farm. Each day it was as though a bit more was being taken away from him - his breath, his work and, eventually, his independence.

Dad hated looking out of the window and seeing jobs he was no longer able to do. Having said that, he never shared his frustrations with any of us. He would think about things, mull things over, but wouldn't always share his thoughts.

One day, on the way back from riding, Dad noticed there were four bungalows for sale in Barkston. Two of the bungalows were in a cul-de-sac. I remember him turning into the road so we could have a closer look. On returning home, he told Mum about the bungalows and suggested she have a look at them on the internet.

I think it was seeing these four bungalows for sale, in what would be our chosen village, that cemented his thoughts - that he should retire from the farm and we should move into one of the bungalows.

So, after viewing two of the properties, we decided to buy the one in the cul-de-sac, The Leas. We purchased the bungalow in June 2007. Mum and I spent about six weeks, along with friends and family, getting the bungalow ready and packing up the farm. On 7th August we finally moved in, Dad retired and my brothers Martin and Phillip took over the farm.

When we moved home I had very mixed emotions. I absolutely loved the farm. I suppose I had imagined being there for a good few years more. I had also never imagined my poor Dad would ever have to leave the farm. Nevertheless, this was the situation. We had a new chapter in our lives, the chance to embrace village life.

I was thrilled we had managed to find a bungalow in Barkston. We had looked at a couple of bungalows in Grantham as well and whilst Mum was happy to move into town, both Dad and I preferred a country village.

Although I loved my farm life, I guess looking long term, there was a part of me that craved that community feel. The idea of having a bungalow was attractive as it would mean I could become more independent.

With no stairs, I could access all our home without having to rely on Mum to help me upstairs or fetch things for me. Being in the village would also give me the option of going to the local shop on my mobility scooter.

Once we got settled into our new bungalow I think Dad was relieved. Although I am sure this was a difficult time for him, he never said. After all, he was born at the farm at Syston Grange and had farmed there all his life.

Shortly after we moved, Dad also decided to give up driving as he was having to rely on oxygen 24 hours a day. With a big oxygen machine in the house, he now needed a portable oxygen machine with him when out and about.

On the home machine, Dad eventually got to the stage where he was receiving six litres of oxygen per minute. Receiving this level of oxygen meant he had to wear an oxygen mask as opposed to a cannula. This was because a large amount of oxygen, such as six litres taken through a cannula, would cause burning to the nose.

His portable machine only held enough oxygen to provide him with four litres per minute. When it came to taking him out for hospital or doctor's appointments, he would go for a considerable amount of time with less oxygen than he required and this took it out of him.

Seeing Dad, my best friend, having to rely on a machine 24 hours a day, to simply breathe, was the worst thing I will ever have to watch. Everything was a struggle for him. He would sit all day in his reclining chair with everything he needed around him, but even reaching out to pick something up required a considerable amount of effort. He loved watching sport on Sky. He was always a big rugby and cricket fan, but some days he wouldn't even have the strength to be interested, and that was hard. That told me a lot about how he was feeling, both physically and mentally. In those moments, I did everything I could to keep his interest in things that were happening. Sometimes it worked and sometimes my efforts failed.

There were days that were so hard for Dad to get through, so much so that I could see him lose his fight. At times, he felt like giving up and he would say that he didn't want to live anymore. As you can imagine, this was so hard and upsetting to hear. I used to get cross with him for saying such a thing. But I couldn't help but understand his shear frustration and the fight he undertook every single day just to be able to breathe.

These days were unbelievably tough, but I just had to keep going - it was my turn to look after him now. I always treasured every moment, every day that I had with him as, in the back of my mind, I just didn't know how much time we had left.

Sadly, over time, it got to the point where Dad had to rely on a wheelchair as walking just took so much out of him.

I used to go with Mum to take Dad to his hospital appointments so I could help her where I could. On occasions, Dad's breathing would get so bad that he would be admitted to hospital. I hated him being in hospital, however there were times when I felt relieved he was in a place where he could be monitored and treated. I used to get frustrated if I thought the doctors hadn't been to see him, or nothing was being done, but I think Dad was always well looked after.

I hated seeing Dad so poorly. Mum and I did all we could to look after him but, of course, it frustrated us that we couldn't do more to make his life more comfortable.

Alongside the fibrosis of the lung, my poor dad had other health conditions to contend with. He had problems with his heart as well as sugar diabetes, both of which worsened as his lung condition deteriorated. For many years, his diabetes was controlled by diet but eventually he had to inject himself with insulin twice a day. When Dad was particularly ill and would be struggling to breathe, his diabetes would be affected and his blood sugar would drop significantly. Often his time in hospital would be about getting his oxygen levels back up and controlling and stabilising his blood sugar levels.

Then in March 2012, Dad began to deteriorate rapidly and was admitted to Grantham Hospital. Early in the morning on Sunday 25th March, Mum and I received a phone call from the hospital. We were told to go and see Dad as he was very unwell. That day, visiting hours didn't apply to us. Mum, Martin, Phil and I took turns to sit by Dad's bedside throughout the day. From the moment we received that phone call, I knew in my heart this didn't sound good. But, I am never one to give up. I still held on to the hope that he would recover, just like he had done before.

I was due to go to France the next day for an international competition and Dad insisted I should still go - the last thing he would have wanted was for me to not go because of him. So, even though I couldn't imagine going to France, I did what Dad wanted and went to the yard that afternoon to pack the lorry. Leaving him was so hard and I made Mum promise she would call immediately if I was needed.

I visited Dad again in the evening. He looked so, so poorly and tired. He just lay there and was dropping in and out of sleep. Mum and I just held his hand and stroked his head. I didn't want to leave him, and I wish now that we hadn't, but the nurse said she would call us during the night if he needed us.

Mum and I went home and spent the night cuddling up on the sofa. Neither of us could sleep. Something told me I shouldn't put my pyjamas on that night and I should stay dressed but, for some reason, I chose to ignore it.

The phone rang about one o'clock in the morning. It was the hospital saying we should get there as quickly as possible.

Heartbreakingly, we didn't make it in time and, on arrival, we were met by a nurse, who told us Dad had passed away.

I was distraught to think we were not with Dad when he died. I blamed myself for not being there. If only I had insisted on staying by his bedside all night, if only I hadn't put my pyjamas on. I wouldn't have had to get dressed which delayed getting to the hospital and, if only I hadn't needed my wheelchair to get to the ward. Basically, if Mum had been on her own she would have got there quicker and would have been with him.

I don't remember when the news eventually sunk in. I do remember going to see Dad though and, amongst the heartache and devastation of losing him, noticing how peaceful he looked. He didn't have any wires or tubes connected to him, nor did he have any oxygen machines or oxygen masks. He looked so peaceful, so free.

The next few days and weeks after Dad's death were unbelievably tough. My trip to France was cancelled. I know Dad would have wanted me to go, but I just couldn't - I couldn't for me, but neither could I have left Mum. I was involved in planning Dad's funeral, alongside Mum and my brothers, and I felt it was important we all had a say in the arrangements.

We had a family service at Grantham crematorium and a memorial service at Barkston church.

The memorial service was big. Dad had so many friends from farming and his sporting days that the church was standing room only and overflowed outside. I felt overawed as I walked into the church. There were people standing up and some sat in the choir stalls.

It was a lovely service. Michael Coney gave the eulogy, which was perfect and covered all aspects of Dad's life, including all his four children. Michael was a family friend and our neighbouring farmer. He and Dad got on very well and would often help each other out. They always enjoyed a laugh and joke together.

Dad was the biggest wind-up merchant and it was Michael who often took the force of Dad's practical jokes. He knew Dad, our family and farming so well.

On the eve of the funeral, I asked my niece and Dad's eldest grand-daughter, Claire, to drive me up to the farm. I wanted to drive around looking at the farm, just like Dad and I used to do. We drove into the 'punchbowl' - a big semi-circular field on a hillside, hence the name. Mum and Dad had always said this was where they would build a house if they could, as the view all over Grantham and beyond is amazing. Claire and I just stopped, looking at the view and reminiscing about Dad - it was a special moment.

It was hard, but I wanted to be on the farm as that was such a special place for Dad and we both shared some very happy times there together. Those happy times are with me every day.

I think Dad would be so proud I have overcome the challenges I have since his death. Though he wasn't one for expressing his emotions, I know how proud he was when I became European and World Champ-ion. And this would be no different with my new career. He would be full of pride knowing that I have spoken at TEDxPeterborough in April 2019 and that I am trying to make a difference as a motivational speaker.

Dad's unwavering love and support has shaped me so much and, to this day, enables me to share messages of hope, resilience and deter-mination, to show people that there really is "No Such Word As Can't". For that I am eternally grateful.

CHAPTER 9

THE PERFECT PARTNERSHIP

My love of horses which, in retrospect, began from the first moment I sat in the saddle as a toddler, has become such a huge part of my life.

There is nothing on this planet I love more than spending time with horses. I love getting to know a horse, learning about them and their unique personalities, spending time with them, feeding them, caring for them and loving them for the amazing animals they truly are.

Those early years on horseback had paid off as my riding skills improved and, by the turn of the century, it was time to up my game.

When I began competing in RDA Dressage competitions in 2001, the ground rules had changed quite a bit. The first thing I had to do was to be classified into a grading profile for competing.

Every disability or para sport runs under a profiling system which allows the athlete or competitor to compete on a level playing field, which is based on the type or severity of their disability.

In RDA Dressage, or in the Paralympic sport of Para Dressage, riders are assessed by two medical professionals such as physiotherapists or doctors. With Para Dressage, one of these professionals must be international.

Riders are profiled into five grades. When I started in the sport, the five grades were 1a, 1b, 2, 3 and 4. Nowadays riders are graded into grades 1 to 5. There are lots of different profiles within each grade covering a vast range of disabilities and impairments. The assessment is carried out by medical professionals. As riders are assessed on their disability, as opposed to their ability as a rider, assessments are carried out off-horse.

I remember being assessed on my core strength, balance and co-ordination. For each test carried out assessors gave me a mark. Total marks for the whole assessment were added together. This put me into a specific profile with each profile made up of one of the five grades.

Because my cerebral palsy affects my core strength, balance and co-ordination, my classification profile, 12A put me into the grade 1A category (now grade 1). My disability is reflected in the level of dressage test I am required to compete in. Therefore, as a grade 1 rider, I compete in walk only tests.

With the Foot and Mouth outbreak in 2001, horses were not able to travel, so my first competition was done via video.

At the time, this was unusual. However, it wasn't long after that the 'dressage anywhere' competitions took off and became very popular within the equestrian world. These competitions give riders of all ages and experiences the opportunity to have a go at a dressage competition, without having to worry about getting to the competition, riding in front of other people or anything else that might put them off competing at another venue away from home.

Even though this was my first dressage competition, it did seem strange not actually going anywhere. The phrase 'getting all dressed up and having nowhere to go' springs to mind. My horse still had to be bathed and plaited, I had to wear my white jodhpurs, white gloves and navy jacket and hat, just as I would have done if I had gone to a competition venue.

My instructor filmed me. The good thing about competing in this way was that I could have more than one go at my test and send the best version to the judging panel. From what I can remember, I had two, maybe three run-throughs. I was nervous with it being my first 'competition'. Looking back now, it was a luxury to be able to have more than one chance to perfect my movements. Usually it is just four and a half minutes and one chance only.

After my test was videoed I sent it off to be judged. I was riding a horse called Linda. Linda was a bay mare and was my instructor's former dressage horse. I was placed first in the junior section and second overall and was thrilled with my results. It felt like a good start in what was a new chapter in my riding.

In 2002, precautions surrounding the Foot and Mouth outbreak had subsided, meaning horses could travel again. I could take part in the North Midlands RDA dressage qualifiers, this time, riding Rosie. Rosie was everybody's favourite pony, a bit like Splash was. She was 14hh and dark bay and was just a great pony to learn on. I remember feeling very nervous in my first competition, but thrilled to qualify for the RDA National Championship held that July at Hartpury College in Gloucestershire.

At this point, I was totally hooked on dressage and, during an RDA competition organised by my instructor, I was spotted by Chris Portafield. Chris was a well-known para judge and suggested I should enter a para class being held at Sheepgate Equestrian Centre, not far away in Boston, Lincolnshire.

I was so excited to compete at Sheepgate. This was my first para class and it was also run alongside able-bodied British dressage classes, so very different from RDA. Here I rode another RDA horse, Flicka. Flicka was the first 'horse' that I rode as opposed to a 'pony'. She was a roan colour (sort of black with a speckled bottom) and stood at about 15.3hh. I always felt very confident on Flicka and had a lot of trust in her.

Whilst at Sheepgate, after competing, I met Jane Goldsmith, coach to the Great Britain Para Dressage Squad. Jane was very encouraging and explained to me about the sport and the Start and Potential programme.

I was very excited, albeit a little nervous, after listening to Jane. I wanted to find out about the para dressage squad and the world class Start and Potential programme and, most importantly, I wanted to know what I had to do to be considered for selection. It was probably a good thing I didn't 'bump into' Jane until after I had finished competing, otherwise I would have been even more nervous, which would have affected my riding.

I remember going home from competition full of excitement, ambition and plans. It was time to know exactly what was needed to get me a place at the Start and Potential selection trial, taking place in February 2004.

The world class Start and Potential programme (now known as Podium Potential) is a developmental programme that identifies riders with potential talent and nurtures and develops them along the performance pathway. The aim is to get them representing Great Britain at European, world and Olympic/Paralympic level. These development programmes are run in the three Olympic equestrian disciplines - eventing, showjumping and dressage, plus the Paralympic discipline of para dressage. The selection process is similar for each discipline.

In February 2004, I received the news I'd been waiting for. My application had been successful. I was on my way to the selection trials for the para dressage potential squad at The Unicorn Equestrian Trust at Stow-on-the-Wold, Gloucestershire.

The selection process was very intense and included riding as well as interviews covering things such as my own goals, equine knowledge and sports psychology.

Before the selection trials, I spent a lot of time preparing at home. I treated it as though I was preparing for an exam. After all, the outcome would dictate my future.

For the riding side of the selection process, I rode Flicka - the roan colour horse I spoke about earlier.

I was required to work my horse in the arena on my own to show I had the knowledge and ability to get the best out of her.

I also had a short lesson with one of the selectors. This was not only another chance for them to test my knowledge and ability, but also indicated to the selector how trainable I was.

The final thing I had to do was to pick two movements out of my dressage tests, ride them and then discuss how the movements went. I did a lot of preparation to develop my knowledge surrounding these two movements.

It was vital that I demonstrated knowledge of the correct aids I needed to be able to ride the movements.

I also had to prove my knowledge of the things my horse could do to get out of the movement or mistakes I was likely to make.

By developing knowledge, I could have an informative discussion with the selectors about what went well, what could be improved and how I could develop the movement.

I remember two interviews which were geared towards goal setting and sport psychology and another which tested my general equine knowledge and the care of sport horses. For these interviews, I did my homework by thinking about what my short, mid and long term goals were within the sport. It also meant revising all of my horse knowledge and care.

I felt I had done my best in both my interviews and riding assessment, but was it good enough? I waited anxiously every day for a week for the postman to arrive. Had I done enough to be accepted onto the programme? Then, it happened. Yes, I had been been selected onto the potential squad. I was thrilled!! Finally, I felt like I had an equestrian career - just what I had dreamed of.

Being on the Start and Potential squad required a lot of commitment from me, my trainer and my parents, but what a fantastic experience.

We had four weekend squad training sessions a year held at the Unicorn Trust. During these sessions, we had lessons with the squad trainers and various appointments with the squad's sports science professionals, both human and equine. Squad sessions also included test riding with guest judges as well as performance analysis screening.

Then in June 2004, I was presented with my first major challenge. I was sent, as part of a squad of three, to represent Great Britain in my first international competition in Madrid, Spain.

This was a borrowed horse competition which meant the luck of the draw as to what horse you ended up with. This scenario was very daunting as I was not only representing my country at international level, but I was also going to be riding a horse I didn't know.

To make the situation even more petrifying, I discovered my draw was a 21-year-old Iberian ex bullfighting stallion called Duque. At this early stage in my career, the words 'stallion' and 'bullfighting' stuck out as being somewhat of a scary proposition. Once I got over the shock, I only had two days training for me to get used to him and him to get used to me before the competition started.

This was a whole new challenge. They say it takes a year to properly get to know a horse and yet I, along with the team support staff, had just 48 hours to a) make sure the horse was suitable for me to ride from a safety aspect, and b) ensure Duque and I understood each other and I could ride my test on him.

For the competition, even though riding a borrowed horse, I took my own tack, including a saddle. You can imagine the look on the faces of the airport staff when we arrived with saddles, boots and schooling whips!

It was pot luck as to whether my saddle would fit my mount in Madrid. However, it was a saddle I was used to riding in, therefore it was worth taking. If it did fit the horse it would be hugely beneficial.

Luckily, the saddle belonging to the borrowed horse was fine and we went ahead.

It was also important for me to have my own reins. They have loops which help me grip. My own stirrups with toe-caps also stop my foot from sliding through the stirrup.

When it came to the competition, I needn't have worried about riding Duque as he was such a lovely chap. He looked after me very well. Even though Duque got less and less enthusiastic as the event progressed, we still came away with a great result. Two first places and a second place. Not bad going for an animal and human partnership forged over such a short period.

I had plenty of support whilst competing in Madrid. Mum and Dad went out with me and whilst there I had two surprise visitors. It was at the end of the opening ceremony when two 'old' ladies popped up from behind a bush. It was Auntie Brit and her friend Grace who had come out to support me and have a holiday.

During my time competing in Spain, I also underwent my International classification, required for competing internationally in the sport. The process of international classification was the same process as that of national classification, the only difference being that one of the classifiers was an international representative. Once again I was profiled as a Grade 1A rider.

In February 2005, I went up for re-selection for the potential squad. Now the squad was tiered into gold, silver and bronze levels for funding, according to their level of potential. I was thrilled to be selected as a gold potential rider.

It was during 2005 I met my current trainer, Angela Weiss. Angela was a successful Grand Prix rider and trainer. She was trainer to the Team GBR Grade 4 multi-medallist, Michelle Crunkhorn. Angela became squad coach for the development squad and, as she was from Nottinghamshire - my part of the world - it wasn't too long before I made the decision to start training with her.

2005, also saw big changes within the sport. Prior to this, the sport was all about the riders' ability as all international competitions were using borrowed horses. Then it became more about the partnership and became more important for a 'good' rider to also have a 'good' horse.

With all this happening, the time had come for me to have my own horse - fantastic news as I had been pestering Mum and Dad for years to let me have another horse.

Searching for a suitable horse for me is somewhat of a marathon challenge, with three key things I initially look for in an equine partner: temperament, quality of the walk and quality or look of the horse.

There are many reasons I focus on these areas.

Let's start with temperament. Besides the general ride ability and train ability of the horse, because of my poor balance it is important any horse I work with is sensible and not sharp or spooky.

Then I consider the horse's walk. Because I compete in walk during all of my tests, my horse needs to have a good quality, correct and loose walk capable of earning high marks in a dressage test.

Finally, the horse needs to be eye catching. They need to look the part and make the judges want to watch our performance.

Over the years I have travelled the length and breadth of the country looking for horses and have even tried 'horse shopping' in Holland.

I bought my first horse, Slightly Welton, known in the stable as Spider, in June 2005. Spider was bred as a three-day event horse and was by the well-known eventing stallion, Welton Crackerjack. Spider competed in novice level British eventing, but his dislike of the bigger fences meant he was unable to progress at intermediate level. I had put a 'wanted' advert in Horse and Hound magazine and Spider's owner replied to it.

Spider was 16.1hh and dark bay, or brown, with just a white sock on one hind leg. When I rode him for the first time, I got a good feeling from him.

When it comes to trying horses, there is always a careful process we undertake. The number one priority is always safety. I always take my trainer with me when I go to look at a horse and I never get on the horse without my trainer trying them first. It is only if she is happy that the horse will cope with my disability, that I will then get on.

When I tried Spider, he was the first horse I had ever tried with a view to buy. Having my trainer with me at every viewing meant she could ask the right questions, look at the right things and was aware of any warning signs that cropped up. She was also able to ride the horses to ensure they were 'safe' for me to ride.

Over the years I have got more experienced and used to what it is that I am looking at and looking for. It has even been known, on a few occasions, for me to go see a horse and, after watching my trainer ride it, decide not to get on. I don't know why, but something has told me, 'no' they won't cope with me… sometimes it's in their eyes, sometimes just a feeling I get. In those circumstances, I just don't risk it.

At this stage in my career, I wasn't particularly looking for a world-beater, but a horse that would take me to the next level - a stepping stone. if you like, between a riding school horse and a sport or competition horse.

Spider was a completely different type of horse to what I would choose now, largely due to the development and difference within the sport. Spider was a thoroughbred and, being bred for three day eventing, he was built more for his speed and stamina. However, it was his lovely loose walk that made him attractive to me.

Nowadays, I would choose to buy a horse specifically bred for dressage, as they are bred to have the characteristics and confirmation needed for the sport. I look for a horse that has what we call an 'uphill' confirmation. This means their shoulders are higher than their back, making it easier to push forward with their hind legs. I also look for a horse with a correct, loose four-beat walk. As I compete at walk only, I need to have a walk the judges will mark high. The horse also needs a temperament which is trainable and accepting of me and different situations.

On viewing and trying Spider and, after having him on a week's trial, we decided to have him vetted. After a clear vetting and a successful trial period, it was a done deal and I decided to buy him. It was an amazing feeling to hand the cheque over for my first competition horse.

I competed with Spider for three-and-a-half years. He was a good move forward in my career. Having just ridden riding school or RDA horses, Spider gave me experience riding a competition horse. We represented Great Britain internationally in France, Belgium and Germany with mixed success.

One of the challenges was that Spider wasn't a fan of big events or prize-givings. I hated competing him at the British Dressage National Championships at Stoneleigh Park, as he just couldn't cope with the electric atmosphere. On those days, my performance goals went out the window as my goal was, just to stay on his back.

The first year at Stoneleigh and Spider was rather 'on his toes' in the electric atmosphere. He managed to keep a lid on everything, until the mounted prize giving. I had a person walking with me on either side to hold him down as we 'passaged' or trotted with a huge amount of energy bubbling over.

The following year Spider and I didn't even make it into the arena to do our test, never mind the prize giving. We were waiting in the shoot

- an area you go to prior to the competition arena. Multi-gold medalist, Lee Pearson, had just completed his test and the spectators cheered. The cheering echoed through the tannoy system that happened to be just above our heads and scared Spider. He turned, shot off and started bucking across the huge warm-up arena.

It was a very scary moment. I just didn't know when or where he was going to stop, or indeed what the outcome would be for me. I couldn't do anything to stop him as, for one thing, all my effort went into just holding on. He was in 'fright' and 'flight' mode. I was rather proud of myself as I managed to stay on for about five 'big' bucks but then I remember the horrid realisation that if he took me out of the arena, we would be on concrete. There was no other option. I decided to let the inevitable happen and I bailed. It all happened in seconds.

Mum had been sat in the stands waiting to watch and video my test. She saw what had happened and rushed to the warm-up arena. Well, I say she rushed, I understand she was a bit hesitant as she was unsure what state she would find me in. She needn't have worried. I was surrounded by paramedics, sat up and laughing. I was fine.

It made me think back to one of my earliest riding experiences. The first time I had fallen off a horse was when I was about four. But falling off Dusty Bin all those years ago was a very different experience. This was my first fall of any significance since then. I suppose I had done well and been very lucky to have avoided any major mishaps. Just like when I fell off Dusty Bin, this incident wasn't going to put me off riding. It did, however lead to making some changes.

Although Spider had been a great stepping-stone for me in my para dressage journey, his inability to cope with the atmosphere at bigger competitions, meant it was time to look for a new partner.

I was looking forward to the proposition of getting a new horse, however, the thought I would have to sell Spider was less attractive. Luckily, I was able to sell him to somebody else on the yard. This was perfect as it meant Spider wasn't going anywhere and I could use the money from his sale to fund my next horse.

At the end of 2007 my search for a new horse began in earnest. This time my search took me to Holland and Belgium. Holland is one of the European countries that is popular for producing quality dressage horses.

I went over to Holland on the overnight ferry from Hull for a two-day whistle-stop tour of the country, shopping for horses. This was a fantastic, albeit whirlwind of an experience. It was great to visit so many amazing yards and watch a variety of different riders train their horses.

One of the horses we went to see was over the border into Belgium. This horse, Sylvano V, was big, standing at 17.2hh at least. He seemed massive and after seeing him ridden I was thinking he was too big and too much of a horse for me.

We watched his owner ride him, my trainer rode him and then I rode him. I admit that I was nervous. I wasn't too sure that I wanted to get on. My gut, for some reason, was saying 'no', but still relatively inexperienced in horse shopping, I ignored it. Maybe it was just his size that was putting doubts in my head? Everyone around highlighted Sylvano's good temperament, so I thought I would look stupid if I didn't at least give him a try.

I got on and he was so well behaved, even coping with a group of children running around and making noise. There was another horse in the arena who was leaping around and Sylvano didn't bat an eyelid.

I went back to try him again the next day as I didn't feel as though I had given him a fair chance. It was after my second trial I decided that, subject to a clear vetting, I would buy Sylvano.

I learned two valuable life lessons from this trip. 1. Always go with your gut instinct and 2, after listening to your gut, never let other people's opinions distract you from it.

My initial gut told me Sylvano, or Sam as I called him, was too big and too much of a horse for me. It turns out my gut was right and on getting Sylvano home it became apparent he could be very spooky. After falling off him a second time, it was decided we couldn't risk it. I had fallen off twice without hurting myself, but it was too much of a risk so we made the sad decision to sell him on.

Just a few days later, my trainer saw a horse advertised on the notice board at our local tack shop, Chandlers.

The horse was local to us at Edenham, near Bourne, Lincolnshire and, after making a call, two days on we went to see him.

This horse's name was Purdy's Dream, also known as Eddie, and was 10 years old. Eddie hadn't done a lot in his 10 years but he appeared to have a very nice temperament and a super walk. He was eye-catching in that he was bright bay with a black mane and tail, a white star on his head, a large white marking called a snip down his nose and a white sock on both hind legs. This was enough, along with his reasonable price tag, to convince me he was worth a go. So, after his vetting, Eddie arrived on the yard.

Within a few weeks of welcoming Eddie, we were put in touch with Graham Worrell, Eddie's breeder. It was lovely as it meant I learned all about Eddie's history. It turned out Eddie had quite a story behind him.

Eddie was a Lincolnshire lad, born on Graham's farm near Gainsborough. Eddie's father was a showjumping stallion that belonged to top Great Britain show jumper, John Whittaker, whilst his mother was a broken down hunter mare who had been destined to be put to sleep. She was named Purdy, hence Eddie's show name, Purdy's Dream.

I always joke that Eddie and I had a lot in common. This thought touches me to this day. Like me, Eddie had a traumatic birth - the only difference was that whilst I had doctors and the best in medical technology to keep me alive, Eddie had a bucket of water thrown over his head to bring him back to life. As we got to know Eddie we also discovered he was rather clumsy and had to be taught about spatial awareness. I used to joke that he too had cerebral palsy - a perfect match!

Eddie was thrown in the deep end of his new career as a para dressage horse. Just five weeks after arriving on the yard, we were to be representing Great Britain in Moorsele, Belgium.

Eddie and I were relatively quick to cement our partnership and during the 2008 / 2009 season were putting 70% plus scores on the door and gradually heading towards the 75% mark. At that time, scoring anything over 70% was considered good and would invariably earn a top placing. Seventy per cent was the threshold we would aim for and 75% plus would be a real achievement.

In April 2009, Eddie and I represented Great Britain in Moorsele once again. Whilst we had a fantastic competition and, on paper, won all three competitions, during the individual class, something from outside the arena made Eddie jump. He shot forward and I lost my balance and fell forwards onto his neck.

With Sylvano, when this happened and I fell forward, he would bolt and I would fall off - but Eddie didn't shoot off, he did something truly amazing.

He stopped and didn't move a muscle. I was clinging on around his neck and didn't have the strength to push myself back up so Eddie just waited. Eventually my trainer came into the arena and helped me sit up again. The judges allowed me to complete my test, even though I had to have outside assistance, something not usually allowed. I completed my test and won my class.

After my test, everybody came up to me and stated 'what a special horse' I had. I knew it, I didn't need anyone to tell me. Having had Sylvano shoot off with me in a similar situation I knew I had found the right partner in Eddie. This absolutely filled me with confidence in Eddie - so hugely important for achieving a successful partnership. I was so, so proud of him and very excited for our future together.

As our partnership and career together went on, situations like this arose again. Just like in Belgium, Eddie would always stop and wait until I either got myself back up, or somebody else helped me up. I can't tell you what this did for my confidence and trust in him. Even if he was 'naughty' or objected to doing something, because I had the confidence in him, I could push forward, 'growl' at him or firmly encourage him with the sound of my voice.

I will never know whether Eddie behaved in this way because he 'knew' of my physical challenges. However, I am a big believer, based on my own experiences, that animals do understand disability. I have witnessed some animals, both horses and dogs, who cope with disability or something 'different' and offer their help and support. I have had dogs in my life that would bound up to me and then suddenly stop, as if they knew they shouldn't jump up at me. Occasionally I've encountered dogs that bark and bark at me which I have always put down to them being fearful of the way I walk.

Based on our amazing track record so far, Eddie had proved himself a good para horse, both in ability and temperament. Our future was so full of promise and I couldn't wait for us to go on this adventure together!

CHAPTER 10

GOING FOR GOLD

A photocall with Purdy's Dream (Eddie) at the end of a fantastic 2009 season.

ollowing a successful 2008/2009 season where Eddie and I were achieving plus 72% at both national qualifying competitions and international competitions, we received our first championship team selection. We were to represent equestrian team GBR at the 2009 Para Dressage European Championships in Kristiansand, Norway.

When the phone call from the para dressage squad performance manager came to say Eddie and I had been selected for the Europeans, I was overwhelmed and so, so excited. I had finally made it onto a championship team... wow!

Being selected onto the team meant I had earned my navy competition jacket with the red collar and large union jack embroidered on the chest - my goal ever since starting the sport in 2004.

I still remember the day this very special jacket arrived in the post. I eagerly un-wrapped it and tried it on straight away. I looked in the mirror with a mixture of pride and excitement. Pride at what I had already achieved to have earned my 'red collar' and excitement at being selected to represent my country at a European championship.

I always felt a sense of pride when wearing any of my team GBR kit, and even today, I feel that same pride when I look at my competition jacket hanging in the wardrobe, or when I wear my polo shirts or coat out on the yard. There is something about that red collar or team GBR logo that will always make me proud of, not only what I achieved, but also what I was part of.

In 2009 Eddie and I were part of a squad of six representing Great Britain at the Europeans. This included a team of four who competed in the team competition and two individual riders. I was an individual rider and was there as the 'new kid on the block' to gain experience at a major championship. I was proud to be competing alongside Sophie Christiansen, Lee Pearson, Jo Pitt, Simon Laurens and Sophie Wells.

Sophie Christiansen and I were both competing in Grade 1A. Sophie was an experienced team GBR rider and had previously won gold medals at Europeans, World and Paralympic Games.

Sophie and I both competed in the individual championship test where there were individual medals up for grabs. I was so nervous as I entered my first championship class with medals at stake.

Somehow, I managed to overcome the nerves and overall I was pleased with my performance. I was so, so excited to discover I had done so well that I'd managed to win the silver medal, just behind Sophie who won the gold! Wow!

The following day was the kur or freestyle to music class. Sophie had said to me the night before she was looking forward to the freestyle as she was the 'freestyle queen'.

Whilst I was warming up for my freestyle, I was oblivious to the fact that Sophie, in the arena before me, had made a few mistakes. My coaches were quietly confident and hopeful that I could do well.

During the freestyle to music you are required to perform a series of compulsory movements. However, unlike the regular dressage tests it is down to you to develop a floorpan that fits around the compulsory movements. You then choose some appropriate music that fits you, your horse and the rhythm of your horse's movement. My test is all in walk, which can make choosing exciting music more difficult.

When selecting pieces of music for freestyle tests there are many things you need to take into consideration. The judges mark your test in two sections. They mark from a technical perspective by marking compulsory movements as they would in the regular dressage tests. They also allocate marks for artistic interpretation and performance.

Timing plays a big part in freestyle to music tests. At my grade, I was allowed between four and four-and-a-half minutes, from halting and saluting at the beginning of my test to the final halt and salute. If you go under or over the time, that's when penalties will occur. I always planned my tests to be around four minutes, 15 seconds to four minutes, 20 seconds - this always seemed a safe bet.

When preparing for a new routine, the first step is to choose a piece of music that matches the beat or rhythm of the horse's paces. Competing only in walk, I must have music with a strong four-time beat that fits my horse's walk rhythm.

When searching for suitable music for the Europeans, I got somebody to video me riding Eddie through the floorplan of my freestyle test and then sent my video off to Lady Inchcape who had been recommmended to me to do my music.

Lady Caroline Inchcape is often referred to as Great Britain's Grand Dame of Dressage and is a breeder, trainer, successful rider and dressage judge.

I hadn't at that stage got any real preferences for my music, so I was happy for Lady Inchcape to make some suggestions.

By looking at Eddie's walk and the overall picture of us as a partnership, Lady Inchcape decided on piano music by Richard Clayderman.

On receiving my CD from her, to be honest, I was a bit sceptical as this wasn't my kind of music and two of the pieces I had never heard. However, I did know the piece from Jesus Christ Superstar, 'I don't know how to love him' and I loved it.

Then, as I rode Eddie to the music, the more I started to love the whole piece. It just fitted us so well.

It is so important for the rider to like the music as it gives you a lift and adds so much to the performance. Believe it or not, the same applies to the horse too. In some instances, it is like you can see the horse 'dance' or stride out to the music.

Then, of course, the judges' preference plays a part. The music needs to make the judges sit up and want to watch. It must add to the performance, as opposed to just being background music. Whilst you can get away with having an odd word in the music, singing is a 'no-no'.

Once you have your music and floorplan, the most important thing is to learn the music. You need to learn it off by heart and I mean totally learn it. You need to know exactly which piece of music is playing at specific points or specific movements throughout the test. This is important for not only fitting specific movements to the specific pieces of music, but also knowing where you are within the whole test - whether you are ahead or behind the music.

When riding a freestyle, a skill you need to acquire is the ability to make split second decisions and changes. Maybe you are ahead of time and need to add in an extra movement, or you might need to take a movement out if you are behind the music, being careful not to take a compulsory one out.

As I came out of the arena after completing my test, I was delighted with how things had gone. It had gone well. My coaches were pleased with our performance too.

It wasn't long before my performance score of 75.5% was revealed. I had won the Gold Medal! Amazing. I couldn't believe it. Eddie and I were European Champions - wow, wow, wow!

I probably shouldn't say this, but it felt amazing to beat Sophie to the gold. So, amazing because, once again, I had smashed another of my performance goals. All these years and I had never quite managed to beat her, but today Eddie and I had done it.

The prize giving gave me the most incredible feeling. When you win any big championship, you usually win a lovely fleece horse rug - this was no exception. Whilst we were waiting to go into the mounted prize-giving, Eddie had a beautiful navy, red and white rug put over him. The rug had gold-piped edging with '2009 Para Dressage European Freestyle Champion' embroidered on the side. I had been waiting to win a rug for years and now, I had finally won one.

Eddie and I led the way into the main arena for the ceremony. Fellow competitors were presented with their medals and prizes and then the announcer said over the tannoy: "The 2009 Grade 1A European Champion is Emma Sheardown and Purdy's Dream". It was very special. The National Anthem played for me as the Union Jack was raised and I was presented with my gold medal, a sash and flowers by members of the grand jury. I was filled with absolute pride and happiness and full of emotion.

This moment was the proudest moment of my life. My dream had been realised. Not only had I represented Great Britain at my first major championships, but I was bringing home the gold.

I also received different prizes from the championship sponsors too - things like Body Shop goodies and woolly socks. Eddie wasn't left out either; he got some horse treats which made him very happy.

As soon as I won the gold medal, I phoned Mum and Dad. I couldn't wait to tell them. Sadly, they were unable to share my European experience as Dad was now on oxygen 24 hours a day and far too ill to come out to Norway with me. Mum stayed home to look after him.

They were both over-the-moon with my win. It was a complete surprise to them, as it was to everyone else.

One of my friends, Emma Kent, who had come over to watch and support the squad, unbeknown to me, had called Mum and Dad so they could hear the prize-giving over the phone and me being announced as European Champion.

I will never be able to thank Emma enough for doing this. This was amazing as it meant that, even though they couldn't be there, Mum and Dad were part of the celebrations, albeit from afar.

Emma's call came as a real surprise. Mum and Dad huddled around the phone to hear my name announced as Grade 1a European Freestyle Champion and the National Anthem played. They had tears of joy and pride rolling down their faces. It was a very special moment for us all.

After Emma had put the phone down, so began the phone calls to spread the news around the family.

What an amazing week! I was so proud to have won a gold and silver medal at my first championships.

I was on cloud nine for ages. I just couldn't believe what had just happened. After the competition, the whole team had a celebration at the hotel, although we had to be up early the next day to catch our flight home.

I remember feeling extremely tired on the flight back, largely down to the sudden drop in adrenaline after the competition was over.

However, the whole team was still on a high as we proudly wore our 'bling' through the airport, on the plane and on the way home. On the flight, the captain announced our achievements to the other passengers. This at the time was a bit embarrassing, but given the fact we all had our medals around our neck, I suppose it was a bit of a give-away.

Once back at The Leas (home), I was met by Union Jacks and congratulation banners. Family members and friends, along with neighbours, were outside my house waiting for me to arrive. It was a lovely surprise. I couldn't wait to go inside and see Dad, who I knew was full of pride, and tell everyone all about my adventures.

Those adventures didn't stop there. In the weeks and months afterwards, I received invitations to attend various events.

One morning I received an envelope with a very familiar logo on. I very excitedly opened the letter to find an invitation to the 2009 Sports Personality Of The Year, being held at the Sheffield Arena. I was so excited.

Mum went to the event with me, whilst one of my brothers looked after Dad. It was a once-in-a-lifetime experience. I was invited to pre-show drinks and the after party. It was great to meet different sports stars, share our successes and collect signatures along the way. One highlight was getting the signature of cricket legend, Dickie Bird. This was special because my Grandad Harry was a big cricket fan.

As my riding career got more exciting by the day, new opportunities were opening up and I couldn't wait to see what was next around the corner.

CHAPTER 11

WORLD CHAMPIONS

Representing Equestrian Team GBR at the World Equestrian Games (WEG), Kentucky, USA in 2010.

During the 2009/2010 season my partnership with Eddie went from strength to strength.

We were consistently increasing our percentages and delivering solid performances.

In June 2010, it was time for the Para Dressage Summer Championships at the iconic All England Showground in Hickstead, Sussex. The venue is famous for the Hickstead Derby - a prestigious show-jumping competition.

In my Grade 1A class I was competing alongside Sophie Christiansen and Paralympic multi-medalist, Anne Dunham. Anne is an amazing person. She started her career as an able-bodied rider before developing a disability. Gradually, as Anne's health deteriorated she has dropped down the grades in para dressage.

I was looking forward to competing against Anne and Sophie. I hadn't had the opportunity since the Europeans to compete against either of them so I was keen to see how Eddie and I would do against them both.

We had two days of competitions at Hickstead.

Since starting in the sport and being selected onto the world class Start and Potential programme, my performance goal had always been to beat Anne and Sophie. I also knew that if I ever stood a chance of being selected onto a championship team, then I would have to be winning against them.

I would sit and watch them ride during training and in competition so I could analyse just what was giving them the edge over me.

I learned many things from both riders. With Anne, I learned about the importance of accuracy. Anne's ability to ride every single stride meant her performance was always polished and she was extremely accurate - every movement she rode with precision.

Although, I had pipped Sophie to gold at the European Championships, in the freestyle to music class, I was still yet to beat her in the team or championship test.

By the time Hickstead 2010 came around, Eddie and I had two years' competing together under our belt and had developed a solid partnership.

At this competition, everything just came together. I knew, when I came out of the arena, I had done a very good test. But, at this stage, beating Anne and Sophie was still a dream and I was very aware both were capable of pulling out some big scores.

As it was, I had nothing to fear. To my absolute delight, I won! I had beaten them. I was speechless. Finally, I had reached my goal.

A mixture of emotions followed; obviously, I was extremely happy, but I was also relieved I had proved myself and my worth on the squad. Not only had our win proved my worth, but it also proved Eddie's ability and potential in the sport, and this meant so much. Needless to say, Eddie got lots of hugs and carrots. After all he was the one who had enabled me to finally achieve my goal.

The other growing excitement was that the timing was perfect. I had timed my 'win' right, ahead of selections for the World Equestrian Games. Things were developing just as I'd hoped.

Winners of the five grades went into the overall championship class which was a freestyle to music competition. For me, it put the icing on the cake when I came second behind Lee Pearson, another para dressage idol of mine.

At the time I entered the sport, Lee and his beautiful dun gelding, Blue Circle Boy, were multi-gold medalists and the face of para dressage. As I was already on a high after winning my class, coming second to Lee in the freestyle championship, was incredible.

Fresh from my latest success, the 2010 season was now about preparing and 'fighting' for selection for the World Equestrian Games (WEG). This time there were seven places on the team and there was stiff competition for one of these precious spots, particularly in the Grade 1A category.

Although Hickstead played a big part in selection, the team for WEG wasn't announced until after the international competition at Hartpury College in Gloucester.

When I was selected for the Europeans the previous year, I had received a phone call from the team manager to inform me of my selection. This time it was different. All short-listed riders had to congregate in one of the classrooms after the competition at Hartpury. This seemed like a brutal way of announcing the team as some riders left the room happy, whilst some left heartbroken.

It was certainly a tense moment. Just like being on one of those reality TV programmes, like XFactor, as you waited for your name to be called out. Were you going or were you going home? It was horrible.

There had been speculation about team selection amongst all the riders and support staff, with everybody trying to second-guess the team. I certainly had different scenarios going around in my head, as I'm sure everyone else did.

Team management announced the team in grade order, beginning with Grade 1A - my grade. I think we all thought they would select two out of the three of us, but who? Anne and Sophie had more experience, but Eddie and I had been beating them, giving us an equal chance of being selected.

We waited. The room was silent with anticipation.

Then the announcement. In the end, and to our amazement, all three Grade 1A riders - Anne, Sophie and I - had been selected. Everyone in the room was visibly shocked.

As the rest of the squad was announced things began to take shape. The 2010 WEG squad would be me, Anne Dunham, Sophie Christiansen (Grade 1A), Lee Pearson, Ricky Balshaw (Grade 1B), Jo Pitt (Grade 2) and Sophie Wells (Grade 4).

Whilst the selected team were all congratulating one another, I felt awful for those who hadn't been chosen. It seemed unfair all the Grade 1A riders had been selected and yet there were no Grade 3s. It didn't feel right. Everybody in that room had put in the same amount of work and commitment and yet they hadn't made it, but I had. I just didn't know what to say.

Amidst speculation and anticipation was concern about three Grade 1A riders being selected. From a performance outcome point of view there was only one gold medal up for grabs, with only one rider potentially achieving gold. If, on the other hand a Grade 3 had been selected, it would have given the team an additional opportunity for gold.

Leaving these concerns behind, preparations for WEG were soon underway. However, it didn't go without some major stresses.

On one morning, Eddie was eager to come in from the field. As he was banging on the gate, he got one of his front legs caught, cutting himself at the back of his fetlock.

Our vet came out to see him and it was decided we should take him to a veterinary hospital. He spent a week there where his wound was kept clean and he received antibiotics. The squad vet kept in close contact with the hospital vet, so we were kept up to date with Eddie's condition ahead of WEG.

Eddie being in a veterinary hospital just weeks before WEG was a complete nightmare. Not only was I worried about his injury, but I was beside myself worrying about him being in an equine hospital, potentially surrounded by banned substances.

What if vets accidentally gave him something that was banned? Maybe they hadn't read his notes properly or, because there were lots of different vets and nurses on duty at different times, what if the message about them having to be careful didn't get passed on? What if the horse in the stable before Eddie had been on a substance that Eddie mustn't have? The stable might be contaminated. It was always on my mind.

I'm sure I drove the poor nurses mad as I explained my concerns and the seriousness of the situation on more than one occasion. Fortunately, as WEG was only a couple of months away, the squad vet kept in touch with the hospital vet to keep up to date with Eddie's progress. This gave me a bit of reassurance that there would be discussions between the two vets about medications and treatment.

A serious consideration and a big part of competing at this high level, for horse and rider, is anti-doping. As both a development and performance rider, I received anti-doping education. I was always extremely careful, in fact maybe a bit paranoid, when it came to keeping my horses safe.

Nobody was allowed to feed them treats or anything without asking. There was no room for error. Carrots were ok, but if it was manufactured horse treats then, just as with different feeds, I would always need to check on the ingredients or with the feed manufacturers themselves to ensure they didn't contain any banned substance. Then, and I am sure it is no different now, there were pages and pages of banned substances - it was a real minefield. Substances banned under the International Equestrian Federation (FEI) include rosemary and caffeine.

Contamination was another issue. It is so easy for substances to be passed, not just through direct contact, but through contamination.

My horses always had their own feed and water buckets, feed scoops and mixing spoons. These were all colour coded and clearly marked with strict instructions, including that they weren't to be used for any other horse. I also put up notices in the feed room and outside their stables, giving clear instructions.

I think some people thought I was slightly obsessive, but I had to be. A positive dope test from me or my horse had the potential to result in a career ban - it was that serious.

On his return home, Eddie had to have box rest to begin with and then was gradually bought back into work. I had our own vet visit him frequently leading up to WEG just to check he could withstand the work required.

From getting him home, we had about six weeks to ensure Eddie was fit and ready.

With hard work and dedication, we managed it. After days and weeks of worry, Eddie was raring to go.

The World Equestrian Games (WEG) were held in Kentucky in the USA. I am not the biggest fan of flying, but this was such an incredible opportunity there was no way this was going to stop me.

I know exactly where my dislike of flying originated from. When I was 11 we went on holiday to Jersey and flew on the tiniest prop-plane ever. It was very small and I felt very 'closed in' inside.

It was so noisy. I had been on bigger, much quieter planes before, but this was an altogether different experience.

I convinced myself something must be wrong with it. It took me the first half of the holiday to get over my ordeal and I spent the second half building myself up to fly home.

I refused to fly again until 2004 when my parents said if I wanted to be on the squad, then I would have to get over my fear of flying. That was the easiest phobia cure ever. Dangle a horse at the other end and I am there!

For WEG we flew as a human team from Heathrow to Cincinnati and then onto Lexington. The horses went by road and the Channel Tunnel to Liege airport in Belgium to fly out to Chicago.

At Liege the runway is longer, giving the cargo plane a more gradual incline on take-off for our horse team mates. Good news for both horses and humans!

During the flight our horses were transported in pairs in crates. This is similar to horses travelling side by side in a trailer. Eddie was paired with Sophie Well's horse, Pinocchio. The squad vet and grooms were on board to look after them.

Arriving in Chicago, the horses spent a few days in quarantine before being transported by road to the competition venue, Kentucky Horse Park.

From the moment we took the horses to meet up with the rest of the team at the Arrow Riding Centre in Dartford, Kent to when they returned after competition, they were under constant observation from the squad's vet and osteopath.

For the duration of the trip, horses were weighed, had their temperatures taken and, twice a day, were trotted up to make sure they were sound. The vet and osteopath watched the horses train and compete. Then they talked to riders, coaches and grooms about any concerns or adjustments for their exercise or feeding regimes. Both professionals were also there to provide any treatment needed.

We arrived in Kentucky on the Wednesday while the competition officially started the following Monday.

It wasn't until the Thursday that I could see Eddie. I couldn't wait to see him and, after such a long journey and new experience for him, I was eager to ensure he was alright. I was pleased to see him well, relaxed and settled in his stable. We were totally ready to compete.

The World Equestrian Games consisted of all eight disciplines - para dressage, dressage, eventing, showjumping, vaulting, endurance, carriage driving and reining.

This was a big moment for the sport and me. It was the first time para dressage had run alongside the able-bodied disciplines. The Paralympic Games are separate from the Olympic Games and, until WEG in 2010, both the world championships and European championships were kept separate from events featuring our able-bodied colleagues.

It was so special that riders from all disciplines could compete alongside each other and share their support. We were one big 'Team GBR'.

Equestrian Team GBR took over a Holiday Inn as the team hotel for the games. Hotel staff were amazing and so were the volunteers who ran the shuttle buses, transporting us backwards and forwards to the venue every day.

Every time the team won a medal, hotel staff would put a soft-toy horse on the hotel reception desk. By the end of the competition, we were even referred to as 'The Magnificent Seven'. It was great.

The whole experience was wonderful. I was in awe having breakfast in the same room as my childhood idols - event riders, Pippa Funnell and William Fox-Pitt, and showjumper, Michael Whittaker. It was so surreal being on the other side of the world competing alongside these amazing equestrian stars.

I still remember clearly when event rider William Fox-Pitt won his silver medal. The fire alarm in the hotel had gone off which meant we all had to assemble outside. William had just come back from the venue, so I could offer him my congratulations. It was quite a special moment.

Throughout the whole WEG experience, I felt immensely proud and humbled to think I had been selected to represent my country alongside these experienced and well-known equestrian celebs.

Once again, Eddie and I competed as individuals for Great Britain and were not part of the team for the team competition. Being an individual meant that, although we could ride through the team test to get into the arena and be judged like everybody else, our score didn't count towards the team.

Although an amazing, experience, the trip didn't go without quite a fair amount of stresses and challenges.

On the Sunday morning, the day before competition, I received a phone call from the squad vet. The news wasn't good. Eddie wasn't sound. The leg he had cut back home was causing problems again. I couldn't believe it. Everything had seemed to have healed nicely and yet here we were in a stressed state, just hours before competition. I didn't understand what was going on.

For a second, I remember thinking we have come all this way and I am soaking up this amazing experience, but I might not be able to compete. I felt helpless. All I could do was put my trust in the team staff to do what they could to help Eddie.

To try and distract myself, I went and explored Kentucky Horse Park - a vast area of beautiful parkland. I went shopping around the various trade stands and bought a pair of cowboy boots. Well, I couldn't go all that way and not bring home a pair, could I? I also used the time to watch the competitions in some of the other disciplines.

The squad vet and squad osteopath, along with the groom, worked hard to treat Eddie and get him sound enough to pass the trot-up.

Although I only compete in walk, my trainer would usually warm Eddie up in all three paces - walk, trot and canter.

This time we had to keep his trot work to an absolute minimum to ensure his lameness didn't get any worse. If we'd carried out Eddie's normal warm-up routine it could have aggravated the injury.

Luckily, with the right care, Eddie was good and we were ready for competition.

When it came to the individual test, Anne, Sophie and I were all in Grade 1A class.

After a tough contest, I was delighted to win the bronze medal. Sophie and Anne won gold and silver respectively. It was fantastic. I had won my first World Championship medal.

From the team point of view, it couldn't have been a better result - a GBR 1, 2, 3!

Unlike the prize-giving at the Europeans, the WEG prize-giving was unmounted and on podiums. However, the horses didn't miss out. They were led in by our grooms and stood just behind us. As my name was called, I stepped forward onto the podium followed by Anne and Sophie.

I remember looking at them with an overwhelming sense of pride and accomplishment. All three of us had taken medals for our country. Seeing the Union Jack raised and hearing the National Anthem played for us all sent goosebumps down my spine and brought a little tear to my eye. This was literally the 'dream'!

After the medal ceremony, and still on a high, the GBR Para Squad had a photograph taken around a statue in Kentucky Horse Park. We posed for a lovely photo which was used on the front cover of the British Dressage magazine.

Life was good in this moment. But then disaster.

As I walked away from the statue, I tripped over a raised light in the ground. I fell face first. I was covered in blood and in so much pain. Everybody ran over to help, but it was too late. The damage had been done. I had broken two of my front teeth. After being checked over by the squad doctor and medics on site, it was decided I needed to go to hospital.

In a strange twist to the story, I was taken to Lexington Hospital in a fire engine with a paramedic called Captain Miracle. Yes, really. I never did discover why he answered to that name. I guess there must be a heroic story in there somewhere. He certainly was my hero on that day.

Anyway, in shock and battling with pain, my trainer and team doctor accompanied me. I can't remember a thing about the journey. I think they put me on a stretcher, as I vaguely remember looking at the outside of the vehicle before being taken inside.

Then I had to wait whilst the emergency dentist was called in. I was given a cotton bud with anaesthetic to put on my teeth to help numb the pain. The main problem was that when the team doctor put the cotton bud anywhere near my teeth, I leapt half a mile. I couldn't stand anything touching them.

Eventually, the dentist arrived and, on examination, confirmed my two front teeth had broken clean off. His job was to put temporary crowns on them. This was easier said than done. Every time he did something to the teeth, I hit the roof. Cerebral palsy makes it difficult for me to keep still at the best of times, but when you add pain to the mix, it's virtually impossible.

My trainer and team doctor were forced to hold me down to keep me still, so I could be treated. I don't know how the dentist managed the treatment, as my broken teeth were so, so sensitive. When I think about it now, I can still feel the pain and get shudders down my spine.

At some point during the night or early hours of the morning, I was discharged and allowed back to the team hotel.

The events of that night were another surreal experience, but for all the wrong reasons. I couldn't quite believe what was happening.

Although I managed to get some sleep, it was a short night as I had to leave the hotel at 8am to go back to the dentist in Lexington for a check-up. We had to be sure that I was okay to compete.

It was the last day of competition for me - freestyle-to-music day - and I was determined I wasn't going to let a couple of broken teeth get in the way.

Luckily my test time wasn't until about four in the afternoon so I went straight to the venue from the dentist. I remember lunch that day was soup. About the only thing I could eat as I could only get liquid down through a straw.

Despite all this going on, it was soon time to warm up for my test. My trainer was restricted as to how much she could do with Eddie in the warm-up, because he was still having leg problems.

It was also another hot day. I so wasn't feeling my best. Lack of sleep, being dosed up on painkillers, the very hot weather - it was all taking its toll.

At one stage, things were so bad I was falling asleep at the side of the arena. To keep me awake, our team doctor and teammate, Sophie

Wells, gave me cola and chocolate to boost my energy levels and kick-start me back into action.

Sophie knew she needed to get me focused ready for my test, so she asked me to recite my test to her. I think I worried her ever-so slightly when I proceeded in a slurred, sleepy voice. "Well, I enter at A and I halt 'somewhere' in the middle". I knew what I meant. I meant that I halted with the music and not at a specific point on the centre line, but I understand that to Sophie, it must have sounded like I didn't have a clue where I was going. She must have thought if I was that sleepy and 'not with it', how on earth was I going to be able to get through my test?

She needn't have worried. I was determined I was going to compete. If I'm honest, there was a point when I thought maybe I can't, maybe I shouldn't. But, I was so close at this point, so, I just went for it! I had to.

I got on Eddie at the last possible moment. In those days, trainers could warm-up horses for Grade 1 and 2 riders for 20 minutes. Then the riders had to be on the horse for at least 15 minutes before the test time. It was time.

I don't think the squad doctor was too happy about me riding. She spent the entire time of the test hiding behind a concrete pillar, so worried I would fall off.

I remember entering the arena and 'wiggling' my way down what should have been a perfectly straight centre line.

Everything felt a bit strange. I didn't feel quite 'with it'. My head wasn't 'with me' and I felt like I was riding on autopilot.

After the centre line and the halt, things seemed to improve though.

It was odd because as I rode through the test, each movement felt good but then, was I getting a real perspective?

The feeling had been spot on. When the results came out, I couldn't have been more surprised. One of the Team GBR staff members told me, that against the odds, somehow Eddie and I had scored 78.5% to win the gold medal.

Sophie Christiansen and Anne won the silver and bronze medals respectively. I just couldn't believe it! I couldn't understand how, with everything that Eddie and I had both gone through, we had managed to deliver a gold-winning performance.

There was a sense of utter pride in both me and my horse, along with total disbelief. Eddie and I were world champions!

I've already talked about my emotions standing on the podium after winning a bronze medal, but standing on the top podium was something else.

The challenges Eddie and I had both faced to reach this point, made it even more special. I felt incredible.

I celebrated my win with teammate, Sophie Wells, who had also had a successful championship by winning three gold medals. We enjoyed a lovely meal, although my menu choice was limited to softer food because of painful teeth.

The next morning, waking up after a good night's sleep, I remember saying to my trainer "I'm a bit worried". "Why's that, Em?" I replied: "Well, I've just won a gold medal and I was on drugs". I was referring to my painkillers, of course, but the squad doctor had dealt with all that and everything was above board. The gold medal was ours and it felt good.

With our mobile phones not working, thank goodness for Facebook Messenger so we could share the good news.

With about a seven-hour time difference between the UK and USA, if I logged on in the evening and my mum was having a bad night's sleep, we would get a brief conversation. I could talk to her about my win and she could check in to see how I was doing after my fall.

After our celebrations, it was time to head home. The flight was during the night and felt endless. We landed back at Heathrow early in the morning and arrived home around 11am. Once again, I received a wonderful welcoming committee of family and friends and a few bottles of champagne. It was time to mark this very special achievement with those I loved most.

Once back, the main priorities were to get me to the dentist and Eddie back to the veterinary hospital.

I was referred to a dentist that specialised in anaesthetics, which meant there was always an option of anaesthetising me if needed. Two months later, I was fitted with two crowns, or 'plastic' teeth as I liked to call them because they are not real.

Eddie returned to the veterinary hospital. When put under general anaesthetic we discovered the problems he'd had in Kentucky were down to his wound becoming infected so it was cleaned out thoroughly.

It took a while for me to settle back into normal life after WEG. I ran on the adrenaline of the whole experience for two weeks and had to deal with amazing highs, but also lots of lows and stresses. On returning home it felt as though my bubble had burst and I felt deflated. Having my teeth and Eddie's leg to sort out gave me a focus, so I guess that stopped me from sinking into some sort of 'post-WEG' depression.

Just like after the Europeans, we were invited to attend different events. At the International Horse Show at Olympia around Christmas there was a parade in the main arena with the whole Equestrian Team GBR from WEG. We were taken into the arena in traps pulled by horses. I was a bit apprehensive about this, as I always say I would much rather be sat on a horse, than be in a trap behind. I always feel you have more control when you are sat on the horse with the horse underneath you.

Despite my reservations, I enjoyed the moment for what it was meant to be - a celebration. After the parade, we were all introduced to HRH Duchess of Cornwall - the patron of the British Equestrian Federation - who congratulated each one of us.

Events like these, just put the icing on the cake of what had already been an incredible experience.

There was also another side of being this successful. I have spoken a lot about anti-doping precautions regarding my equine partner. However, the seriousness of the situation and the precautions we had to take were no different for me.

If I needed to go to the doctors and was prescribed some medication, I would always check it out with the squad doctor before I picked up my prescription.

After WEG, I was selected to be part of the Whereabouts Scheme. This was a scheme run by UK Sport which required on-the-spot dope testing from selected athletes.

I was required to tell UK Sport where I was going to be for one hour every single day of the year. Mostly, I gave them the time of 6am to 7am at my home address. If, however, I was going to be away, then I would have to inform them of the different address and my selected time.

In a whole year I was fortunate in that I didn't receive a knock at my door, but it was always a possibility. I looked at it as a necessary, but small price to pay to keep our sport clean and healthy. A view I still hold today.

CHAPTER 12

ACTION STATIONS AND MORE MEDALS

I n 2011 Eddie and I had recovered from the drama of the World Equestrian Games and were back to full fitness. To cap it all, we were enjoying another successful season, continuing to achieve high scores in our dressage tests and more wins at national events.

When it came to selection for the 2011 European Championships, to be held in Moorsele, Belgium, I knew selection was going to be tough. For WEG 2010 there were seven riders selected for team GBR, for the Europeans there were only five places. With two less places on the European team, they wouldn't select all three Grade 1A riders. As it was still tight at the top between Anne, Sophie and I, it was hard to speculate which one of us would be left behind.

I knew the outcome would almost be a flip of a coin, I kept thinking of the different combinations and trying to, once again, second-guess who the selectors would choose. I knew I had more than proved myself at WEG, but I also knew Anne and Sophie still had more experience under their belt.

Although I played both scenarios out in my head, I was gutted when I heard Eddie and I had missed out on selection. I took the news hard. The Europeans were the final step before London 2012 and by not being selected, I had taken a step back in my campaign for the home games.

But it wasn't all doom and gloom. Eddie and I had, however, been selected as first reserve. It was a good consolation.

Being a reserve horse and rider combination meant Eddie and I had to prepare as if we had been selected onto the team and were going. However, the chances of getting to the Europeans were very slim. We would only get to compete if something drastic happened to another member of the team.

It was a tough time, not knowing where things stood. I had to pack and get everything ready just in case I received a call up so I did just that. I was given a metal tack trunk, just like all other members of the team. This trunk was to store all mine and Eddie's equipment. We would pack as much as we could so it would be easy to put on the lorry transporting squad horses and all the feed, hay, haulage and equipment.

In my trunk, was all of Eddie's tack, rugs, boots and bandages, grooming kit, as well as my riding hat, boots, etc. Basically, the trunk would be like a travelling tack room.

As for all these, trips, I would have to take enough of Eddie's feed, haylage (an alternative to hay) and supplements to cover him for the duration of the trip, always with a little bit extra, just in case. All my equipment, trunk, bags of feed, haylage and water buckets and mucking out equipment would all need to be clearly labelled with my name.

Horses got dedicated travel containers too. It was vital for the journey.

As team horses were transported together with an allocated groom, the driver and squad vet and osteopath, would pack a travel bag for the horses. This included anything they might need, such as rugs, a spare lead rope or set of shoes. It also included feeds which I would pre-prepare in plastic bags. The bags of feed would be labelled with Eddie's name, morning or evening and any additional instructions. I would also send an instruction sheet with Eddie which would provide the grooms with any information they needed about handling and caring for him.

When packing to go away to any competition, I always had my checklist. It included everything I needed - for me and my horse. I would then tick off each item as soon as it was packed. I liked to pack everything myself as far as possible, so I could double, triple and quadruple check I had everything needed.

On the day, the team were due to meet at Dartford, ready to travel to Belgium, I had to be packed and ready to go too. It got to about 5pm, when we were thinking about turning Eddie out in the field, and the phone rang. It was the squad manager. One of the team horses was lame and I was required to step forward onto the team. This caused a mix of emotions. I was pleased and excited to go to another Europeans and defend my European title from 2009. However, I felt very sad and disappointed for the rider who had to withdraw from the team. It must have been heartbreaking.

As we were all packed, within half an hour, we were loaded up and on our way to Kent. It was dark when we arrived at the Arrow Riding Centre. However, all the team staff, Angela and Sophie were on hand to help pack my equipment onto the big lorry.

After all the rushing, and getting everything sorted out, a good night's sleep was essential. The next morning, I met the rest of the team over breakfast. It was time to focus and come to terms with the fact I was on my way to the Europeans.

The European squad for this year was now me, Anne Dunham, Natasha Baker, Debbie Criddle and Sophie Wells. I was very proud when I was named as a team rider for the team competition alongside Anne, Deb and Sophie. This was the first time I had been on the team. At both the Europeans 2009 and WEG I rode as an individual. I loved this new development.

Breaking my teeth at WEG and then going on to win gold certainly got me a reputation. On my arrival in Belgium, along with a team welcome, our Performance Director, Will Connell, joked he was going to knock my teeth out with a baseball bat, so I would win gold!

My teammates never let me forget the WEG 'incident' either. Every time that I so much as wobbled or slightly over-balanced, they would say "don't fall over Emma". My teeth were the subject of many laughs for ages and all in good team spirit.

During the 2009 and 2011 Europeans and World Equestrian Games, I was lucky to be part of three amazing teams. As a team, we all knew each other well, having worked and socialised at squad training sessions and other competitions.

Whilst we all enjoyed a laugh and joke during the social side of competitions, we all knew and respected each other's pre-performance routine. We knew when to support one another and when to give each other space. For me, it was the support and respect that helped build and maintain a strong and successful team.

For this competition, Anne and I were competing in the Grade 1A class. With London 2012 Paralympic Games just one year away, everyone was even more determined to deliver solid performances, and get on that podium.

Anne was certainly no different and rode every step as though her life depended on it. I am not saying I didn't ride well - I did - I was extremely pleased with my performance, but unfortunately for me, Anne left nothing to chance and was determined she was going to beat me.

In the team test, of course, Anne and I were both riding for the team. The focus for both of us was to ensure we delivered two good percentages. Anne won the team test and I was second. With these performances, both of us had achieved solid scores to count towards the team competition.

In a team competition, results are decided by taking scores for each of the four team riders from the team test and individual test. The rider with the lowest mark is dropped.

I was so happy and proud my scores counted and helped Team GBR to Gold!

In the Individual test, although scores counted for the team competition, Anne and I were also competing for individual medals.

When it came to the kur, or freestyle to music, I had a goal with a slightly different 'twist'. I wanted to win gold, but in aiming for this, I was defending my European title.

However, Anne had other ideas. After another 'masterclass' of a performance, she took the crown from me. I was disappointed not to regain the title of Grade 1A European Freestyle Champion. However, in my view, there was nobody better to hand it over to.

Overall I was happy with my performance. Considering I was on the reserve list for the Europeans 2011, it was another amazing championship for me and the rest of the team. Team gold, individual silver and freestyle silver, bringing my total medal count to three gold medals, three silver medals and one bronze medal. A pretty good medal haul to bring home from three major championships.

To put the icing on the cake, after representing Great Britain on three championship teams, there was another lovely surprise awaiting me.

I received a letter telling me I was to be presented with the British Equestrian Federation's Medal Of Honour for services to equestrianism. I was stunned by this. I couldn't believe I was receiving this Medal Of Honour for a career I absolutely loved. I felt hugely proud.

The British Equestrian Federation's Medal Of Honour recognises activities connected with international endeavour in relation to equestrian sports and is awarded for outstanding services to the British Equestrian Federation or one of its member bodies. The award goes back to 1949 and its role of honour consists of many, many equestrian stars. I felt truly humbled and delighted to be included. It's an amazing honour which I'm still immensely proud of today.

I received my Medal Of Honour alongside fellow para dressage rider Natasha Baker, dressage riders, Charlotte Dujardin and Emile Faurie and showjumper, Robert Smith.

The presentation took place at the Olympia International Horse Show at Christmas.

I loved this show. Mum and Dad took me several times as a child and I loved going as it was always a magical atmosphere. The show is packed full of all things equestrian - from top class showjumping competitions to Shetland pony grand nationals, and it always ends with a spectacular festive finale.

My Medal Of Honour was to be presented, in the main arena, by Andrew Finding, Chief Executive of the British Equestrian Federation.

At this stage in my life, I felt immensely proud I had achieved so much for my country in the sport I so loved. It was such a wonderful experience to be awarded in this way, surrounded by friends and so many equestrian stars and, of course, my mum! Mum had missed out on seeing me win my medals, so I was thrilled she was at the presentation. Sadly, Dad was too ill to attend and stayed home with one of my brothers.

These days My Medal Of Honour lives with my world and European medals at home. I often take them with me when I do motivational talks. Every time I get them out I am reminded of all I have achieved and what amazing experiences I have had.

For quite some time, due to my disability, having an equestrian career seemed to be just a distant dream. The idea of any career or life with horses was, quite frankly ridiculous. Yet, here I am today, with seven medals and a medal of honour for service to equestrianism. It's an amazing feeling.

Back in 2011, whilst I was on a high enjoying every second of my para dressage career, all the time I couldn't get Dad out of my head.

By this point, his health was deteriorating more and more and I would return home from competing or celebratory events, never quite sure what the situation would be like. During my time at home, I would do what I could to help and support Dad and Mum.

Christmas 2011 soon came around and we spent it at home, the three of us. I remember keeping everything quiet for Dad. Mum and I did all we could to make it as special a time as it could be. We'd learned our lessons the previous festive season.

We invited my three brothers and wives for a drink, as I thought it would be nice for Dad to have his boys together. However, it proved too much for him. I felt awful as he was quite poorly for a few days after.

And this was the bitter sweetness of it all. Huge celebrations and success in my wonderful equestrian world contrasting with growing sadness in my home life.

All this and the promise of London 2012 just around the corner.

CHAPTER 13

PARALYMPIC DREAMS

2012 was the year I had been waiting for. However, all my hopes of a fantastic year, very sadly turned into the most challenging year of my life.

I still clearly remember the day it was announced the Olympic and Paralympic Games of 2012 were going to be held in London. I was representing Great Britain at the Festival of Dressage at Hartpury college in Gloucestershire back in July 2005.

This was my first international competition riding Spider. I was very excited. I'd finally got my own horse after years pestering my parents and I was representing Great Britain with him.

On hearing we were focusing on London 2012, although I don't remember specific conversations, I do remember my teammates and I were all excited. Now we could aim to compete at a Paralympic Games on home turf.

At this stage I was just about to start my final year studying animal management part-time at Riseholme Campus. However, having been re-selected on to the potential squad at the beginning of 2005 and recently purchasing my own horse, I had significantly increased training sessions and was spending much more time at the yard.

I was only studying two-and-a half-days at college, so, this meant I could work on my assignments and carry out work experience at the vets on my days off, plus ride and have training sessions on these days.

2005/2006 was a busy year, but I loved the challenge of striving to succeed in both areas of my life.

Mum and Dad had committed to supporting me from the beginning of my career in 2004 and, after the announcement, were even more dedicated to supporting me in getting to London. Even when Dad was very poorly, I was very lucky they still found ways around things so they could help.

It was every British athlete's goal to compete in London and I was certainly no exception. From that day in 2005, the goal, the focus was London. Apart from looking after Dad, everything else revolved around London 2012.

To represent Great Britain in my first Paralympic Games on home soil would be totally amazing and I was ready for it.

As the years went by and London got closer, the dream of representing Great Britain in Greenwich Park got more and more real. I used to imagine myself standing on that podium and, during tougher times, it was this that got me up in the morning.

Although there was a lot of hard work to be done to earn a place on the team, the success Eddie and I had during the three years leading up to London gave me hope that we had as good a chance as anybody else of being selected.

In the four years I'd worked with Eddie, he had achieved so much. When I first bought him back in 2008, I used to say he looked like a cow! Poor Eddie, but as he had not done a lot of work before I got him, he was lacking muscle and his hips did look like a cow's hips. To be honest, at that stage, although he had the walk, the seemingly good temperament and the presence, I didn't know what the outcome would be.

In the end, I couldn't have hoped for better. From his arrival, he had not only become a very special Grade 1A dressage horse, but also European and World Champion. I so wanted Eddie to have the chance of winning a Paralympic gold medal, as it would put the icing on the cake for both mine and Eddie's careers.

Paralympics GB only had five places for the para dressage team, so selection was going to be tough. Having clocked up good results, both in national and international competitions during the 2011/2012 season in accordance with the selection policy, I was so pleased to receive an email from the Squad Manager telling me that Eddie and I had made it onto the shortlist. This was the penultimate step towards being selected onto the London 2012 team. I couldn't have been happier. That gold medal was a step closer.

However, what I didn't know was that fate had other ideas. After battling ill health for months my dad died in the March. I was devastated. Life would never be the same again. It was an immensely sad and difficult time.

To make things even more challenging, whilst I was still grieving and trying to come to terms with Dad's death, the relationship between my trainer and I broke down.

This all started about three weeks after Dad died, when I was competing at the British Dressage Winter Championships. Some people might have thought it was too soon to be back competing after losing Dad, but the championships were part of the selection process for London, so I didn't want to miss them.

Although I was determined to get on with the job at hand, underneath I was still grieving. Probably no surprise then why I delivered a less than satisfactory test. When I got out of the arena, my next challenge started. My trainer made it clear that she was not happy with me. Other people noticed and spoke to me about the way in which they saw me being treated. Aware of my challenging circumstances, they were so supportive.

The relationship between my trainer and I continued to deteriorate. I felt confused, my confidence was at an all time low and, with everything else that had been happening, I went into breakdown.

The weeks that followed were very tough. I wanted to keep going, I needed to keep going. I wanted to go to the yard to make sure Eddie was alright and I needed to train.

As the weeks went by things got worse and I slipped deeper and deeper into depression. One day I went on the yard as I was meant to be having a lesson on Eddie. I was very stressed and not looking forward to going, but I needed to ride as I was due to take Eddie to Angela Weiss's yard for a week whilst my trainer went on holiday.

Angela was my squad trainer, but I also worked regularly with her at home too. On arriving on the yard that day, I remember going over to Eddie's stable and was visibly shaking. I just felt like a complete bag of nerves. I clung onto Eddie's stable door to stop myself from falling over. There was no way I was well enough to ride.

I just didn't know what to do. I needed to ride, I needed to train, I needed to focus on London, but instead of focusing on training, I was now fighting anxiety and depression and feeling that my relationship with my trainer was destroyed.

A couple of days later, with my trainer on holiday, I took Eddie over to Angela's for my week's training.

I couldn't wait to get there, although I did question whether it was worth going as I was so low and ill. Not being able to ride for two days beforehand wasn't ideal preparation for a week of intensive training.

I am so pleased I went as it turned out to be a positive breakthrough. Within a couple of days of being there, I began to relax and become more like my usual self. Angela's grooms were and still are amazing. Always there to help me when needed, but otherwise just let me get on with it and let me try, and that means the world.

During my first lesson, I explained everything to Angela and remember saying: "I don't know how I'll ride as I haven't ridden for a week". I needn't have worried as it didn't take me long to relax and re-focus on the job at hand.

As the week went on, there was a vast improvement in my mental health and my confidence. By day four, I spoke to Mum about the practicalities of staying at Angela's. We lived an hour away, so I knew it was a very big ask for Mum to commit to taking me to Angela's every day. However, I think because of all the problems with my trainer at home and then seeing how I had settled, Mum agreed I should stay. I was so delighted.

The next day, I asked Angela and her mum, June if I could stay. Angela and June agreed and welcomed me to the yard. Mum committed herself to driving an hour to and from the yard most days, instead of what had been just 10 minutes down the road.

Another fantastic plus was my teammate from the squad, Sophie Wells, was also based at Angela's. Sophie took over Eddie's training and often helped me with my riding too. Sophie and I always worked well together as a team as we shared the same work ethic and commitment. For both of us, horses and training were priority above anything else and we had the same attention to detail.

With selections for London coming up, we gave each other support and encouragement. We would share expenses for grooms, go to the gym together and simply help and support one another.

Those first couple of months at Angela's in the run up to selections for London were extremely busy, but I loved every single second.

I learned loads from Angela and Sophie. I would sit for hours watching them riding their horses or watching Sophie have lessons with Angela. I felt so lucky to be at a yard where everything focused on dressage. Every day was like boot camp, which was exactly what I needed - positive and constructive coaching and learning.

As has always been the case through my life so far, riding has been my go to place, the place where I feel the most at home, content, where I can be myself and be free. Through the dark days that followed Dad's death, riding gave me purpose and a reason to get up in the morning.

London 2012 meant everything to me. So, when the selectors decided I wasn't in the right frame of mind to take on such a big challenge like the Paralympic Games, it felt like a true killer blow.

I was gutted my name had been taken off the shortlist. I had worked so hard for years to get to this point. To be told this news just one week before the final selection trials at Hartpury Festival of Dressage was utterly devastating. I was still focusing on my training and preparing for Hartpury, so for them to make this decision without knowing how I truly was, was hard to comprehend.

Obviously, I had no choice other than to respect their decision. However, I felt then and, to this day, they were wrong. I was still extremely focused on continuing my paralympic journey and I believe training and competing would have helped me through those first few months of grief.

My training for London had always given me something to focus on. It was a positive, as I was doing it for Dad. Dad had given so much and had been so influential in my riding career. He had supported me in my bid for selection for a Paralympic Games, so I wanted to compete in London, not just for me, but for him. I still wanted the chance to fight for my place on the squad, but to have that opportunity taken from me was gutting.

I was at rock bottom. Devastated. Raw.

But then I did what I had always done. I thought of Dad. What would he have said? He was a very reasonable sort of person. He was good at seeing things from the points of view of different people. So, whilst he would have been very disappointed and upset at me being removed from the shortlist, I think he would have understood the selector's concerns. However difficult this situation was to accept, I had to come to terms with the decision to be able to move on.

I was pleased that although I wasn't selected to compete in London, I could enjoy the games as a spectator. I went along with some family members and friends down to Greenwich to watch the para dressage and Team GBR in action.

It was so important I went to support my teammates and I also wanted the opportunity to experience what a Paralympic Games was truly like.

Once all the hype of London was over, I very quickly settled back and re-focused on my next goal, the Europeans in 2013. That's how it worked really. Once one championship was over, attention was quickly shifted onto the next goal. It was that drive to be successful again, the drive to get to the next championship that helped me through the disappointment of London. I knew I would never give up. I loved my life and I loved my horses too much to do that.

After three years of travelling to Nottinghamshire four to five times a week, in 2015 Mum and I moved to Nottinghamshire to be nearer the yard. We bought a little bungalow in the nearby village of Ravenshead.

Moving to Nottinghamshire was a big decision as we were moving away from the whole family. However, we decided travelling back to Grantham once a week to see relatives would be easier than travelling virtually every day to Nottinghamshire to ride.

As with the previous house move back in 2007, I had mixed emotions about the relocation. I was excited to be moving nearer to the yard, nearer to Eddie and nearer to my new friends. However, I was sad to leave our bungalow in Barkston and it would be strange moving away from those closest to us.

Although it was Mum's suggestion to move, it was a big commitment for her to make, to move away from her family. I will always be extremely grateful to her for making that commitment.

Moving to Ravenshead meant I could spend more time with my horses, more time training and more time learning from watching Angela ride and teaching other people. It was all the extra time spent with Angela in this environment that has helped me become the rider I am today.

I love spending time at the yard. The girls always let me try to do things. If I can do it, then great but, if I make a hash of it, then we just laugh about it. I am always sensible. I know my limitations and what is 'safe' for me to have a go at and what's not. I just love and appreciate having the opportunity to do the things I have always wanted to do with the horses.

For most people mucking out is a horrible job, but for me, simply by being allowed to get on and do it … I just love it! It probably takes me at least twice as long as everybody else to muck one stable out, but I can do it. I'm lucky the girls don't worry about how long it takes me and appreciate what I can do.

Pushing the wheelbarrow is always dodgy - picture the scene; a 'wobbly' Emma trying to balance a one-wheeled wheelbarrow full of horse poo. Yes, there have been times when me, the wheelbarrow and the poo have ended up in a heap on the floor. At my previous yard, I was always told "you can't do that!" - so having the opportunity to prove there is a way for me to be able to achieve what I want to, means the world.

I also make the feeds up, ready for tea and then breakfast the next morning for all horses on the yard. This can be complicated at times as all the horses have different feeds, different quantities and different supplements. Each horse has their own diet, based on what they need to be healthy and fit for the level of work they are doing.

I just love being on the yard and am always talking to the horses… I'm sure some people think I am mad. I particularly love feed times when all the horses poke their heads over the stable doors and whinny as they wait for their feed. I often put my head over the stable doors and watch them eating. I just love watching them in their stables, especially on a dark winter's evening. Everything is so quiet and still and the horses are all tucked up in their cosy winter PJs (rugs). All you can hear is the horses munching as they eat their tea and hay.

In contrast, I also like to be on the yard on a warm, sunny day. It is always lovely after a long, hard winter to see the horses out in the field, enjoying the grass without having to wear their cumbersome winter rugs.

There have been many funny moments during my training to be a 'groom'. One event with Eddie springs to mind. I was getting his feed out of the feed bin opposite his stable, I had a scoop of feed in my hand when Eddie nudged me, I wobbled and flung the feed over my shoulder and into his stable… that was one way of feeding him!

I have so many lovely memories of time spent with Eddie in the yard and during our training together.

But the clock was ticking and change was on its way.

CHAPTER 14

WOLFIE

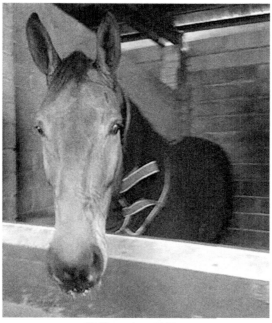

Wolfie, my beautiful boy

By 2013 Eddie was 15 years old. Sadly, it was time to re-evaluate and think about the future. Whilst at that age Eddie would, all being well, have many years ahead of him, he was beginning to show signs of aches and pains. I knew it was time for him to step down from his role and into a slower pace of life. Eddie had done so much for me in a relatively short space of time, so retiring him from his para dressage career at this point was the right thing to do.

In an ideal world, I would have loved to have kept him and just reduced his work. He was my 'golden boy' and will always be extremely special to me. The thought of letting him go was unbearable. However, there was no way I could afford to keep Eddie as well as buy and keep his successor so a decision was needed.

I had to decide whether to sell Eddie or put him out on loan. Initially, the latter option was chosen as it would mean somebody else would have him, look after him and ride him, but he would still be mine and I would have an element of control in what was happening to him. Then I realised that if the loanee sent him back for whatever reason, I would be in the same situation again. There was a lot to consider - so much so that eventually, reluctantly, I concluded the best option was to sell him. Only to a good home, of course.

I wanted a home for Eddie where he could still work and maybe compete at a low level but not be pushed to do higher level dressage movements which would put more stress on his body.

I was very lucky to find Eddie a fantastic new home. Eddie's new owner, Claire, is lovely. She keeps in touch and has even been known to ask my advice about him and his future, which I am so grateful for.

I was so worried about finding a good enough home for my 'golden boy', but I am so lucky, it couldn't have worked out better. I am happy knowing he has such a lovely new family and home.

With Eddie settled, my search for a potential 'Rio partner' began in the summer of 2013. David Hamer, then co-ordinator for the Para Development Squad, told me about a horse for sale at Richard Barrett's' yard in Hampshire.

I went to see this horse with the rest of my team - Angela, Sophie and Mum - and what I saw blew me away.

Beowulf, aka Wolfie, was a young horse, at just six-and-a-half years old, 16.1hh and dark bay. He was gorgeous.

He looked so sweet and my kind of horse. Being tall, my mum always says I look better on a bigger horse, like Eddie who was around 17hh.

However, I don't know why, but there is something about smaller, compact horses I love and, being just 16.1hh, Wolfie, was ideal. There is also something about dark bay horses for competition. Wolfie had two white socks on his hind legs and looked so smart.

I still clearly remember our first meeting. Wolfie was tied up waiting for me to view him. I walked over and carefully went to say 'hello'. He stood quietly as I stroked him and seemed very calm, which to me was another positive.

Sophie rode him for me first so she could check out a few things. During this time she got a feeling for Wolfie's temperament as well as his trainability. She 'wobbled' around a bit to mimic my unruly body to check his reaction and whether he could cope with it. She also tested whether he would be happy having a leg brought over the front of the saddle to dismount, as this is how I have to operate.

I then got on. We took everything slowly, as we always do with a new or different horse. It is not just me getting used to them and the way they feel but also, as I am more wobbly and jerky than other riders, they have to get used to me and feel confident. Thankfully, Wolfie adapted well to the situation and our first ride together was positive.

Wolfie had excellent breeding. His father, Breitling was a well-known successful dressage stallion. He also had a correct four-beat walk with a big overtrack. This means the footfalls from the hind legs land beyond the footfalls of the forelegs.

As I compete in walk only, it is important I have a horse with a 'good' walk. Wolfie's big, correct walk made him an ideal candidate for me. Although we had only had a short time with Wolfie, his temperament seemed laid back, but responsive.

Having a horse with a calm attitude to life is important due to my poor balance. However, I didn't want a horse so switched off that it didn't respond to what I was asking of it. Wolfie fitted the bill perfectly and so I decided I would buy him.

Before this he was examined by a vet - a normal procedure when purchasing a horse.

As he was going to be my next competition horse, I decided to have some x-rays taken, just as an extra precaution. I was so relieved he passed the vetting and had clean x-rays and was so happy and excited when he arrived home at the end of November.

The day after his arrival, Sophie got Wolfie out to exercise him. She put him on the lunge - a long lead rein that allowed the horse to work in a big circle around her. I remember thinking 'wow' as this young horse with loads of talent, sprang around the arena in the most amazing, elevated trot. I was so, so excited to think he was mine. I couldn't believe it was possible to have a horse with this much talent and, at this young age, so much potential.

I spent lots of time in the stable with Wolfie. I love spending time with my horses anyway, but I am also a firm believer that the time you spend around the horse in the stable, either grooming them or just stroking or talking to them is so important for building a partnership.

Just like with riding him, I took everything very slowly with Wolfie. I spent a lot of time watching him so I could see how he reacted to things. Eventually, I would go into the stable with him where I would be extremely careful not to over-balance and startle him. I wanted him to get used to my 'wobbles', but I didn't want to make him jump and scare him.

As I got to know Wolfie, now shortened to 'Wolf', on the ground, he began to respond to me and would come over to be loved. It was as he allowed me to get closer to him that his amazing, kind-hearted, laid back temperament became more and more apparent. It got to the stage where I was able to do things with Wolf I had only dreamed of being able to do with my horses in the past - the things my disability had previously stopped me from doing, largely due to safety.

Up until this point, I hadn't been able to put a head collar on a horse before or put their boots on. This was partly for safety reasons. Being in the stable with them and not being able to move quickly if they moved or if something startled them and made them jump, was not good. Also, I didn't have the co-ordination needed to do up the buckle on the head collar or hold the boots on the leg with one hand whilst I did the velcro up with the other. However, Wolfie changed all of that. He turned 'can't' into 'can' for me as he would stand like a rock for me whilst I fiddled around with buckles and velcro fastenings.

Wolfie had made all my dreams come true. Standing so still for me meant the world and I felt so grateful to him for enabling me to achieve these life-long ambitions.

This milestone meant I could start getting him ready myself. I would go in his stable, put his head collar on and tie him up. I would groom him and put his boots on ready for the girls to come and put his tack on. There were a couple of occasions when I managed to put his bridle on too, although it was fiddly as I had to put the bit in his mouth. Putting the saddle on was one thing I never even tried as they are so heavy and cumbersome. For an able-bodied person, tacking up would probably take 10 minutes, but for me doing what I could, it took much longer due to the co-ordination needed.

I felt lucky the girls on the yard were so encouraging and always celebrated my victories with me. We would laugh along the way when things didn't quite go to plan.

One day, something amazing happened. Sophie was going to ride Wolfie. Whilst she was talking to the girls in the tack room, Wolfie had already been tacked up so I decided to go down to his stable ready for Sophie to arrive. I went into his stable, took his head collar off and said to him "what are the chances of me being able to lead you down the yard to Sophie?" The girls shot out of the tack room as they heard clip-clop on the yard and assumed a horse had got out. Instead (in their words) they saw me wobbling down the yard with a big grin on my face whilst Wolfie walked behind me, being very careful where he put every step.

It might sound silly to an able-bodied person, but being able to do these things with Wolfie meant everything. I was so, so proud of both of us. It was like winning a gold medal all over again. I had done something else that, again, I never thought possible. To me, this was a real positive in the development of our partnership.

When it came to riding Wolfie, that was a different challenge. For one so young, Wolf had an amazing temperament. However, at six-and-a-half, he was still maturing and growing in muscular stature. As he wasn't yet completely developed and able to support himself, when it came to having a rider on his back, he was quite wobbly and needed the rider to help support him. I was very lucky to have Sophie training him. She could give him the physical support needed whilst working on developing his strength and building his muscles up.

Whilst Sophie was building Wolfie's strength, this brought about a few new challenges for me. Imagine a wobbly Emma riding a wobbly Wolfie. We would go everywhere other than where we were supposed to. I can remember going up the banks in the arena, stepping over the arena boards - it was just not happening!

I had learned so much and my riding had developed so much since being based with Angela, but it soon became apparent I would need to up my game even more if I was going to succeed with Wolfie.

The main problems were my balance issues and being weaker in my core strength. Because Wolfie was a more sensitive horse, if I slipped very slightly, either to the right or left in the saddle, he would respond and 'fall' or move with me, hence the reason why we ended going up the banks. This was where more gym work and biomechanics work was needed, as well as lessons on other horses, which played a vital role.

It took a long, long time for Wolfie and I to form a ridden partnership and I did question, at times, during the summer of 2014 whether this amazing little horse was just too good for me. But I had so much love for him by now I was determined to do whatever it took to form the same partnership ridden that we had on the ground.

And this is where 'Grandma Netty' played a vital role. Netty is owned by Val Green and is a livery on Angela's yard. At that stage, Netty was 24 and a poppet of a horse. Angela would teach people on the lunge on her - she is a proper schoolmistress. Val had very kindly said I could ride Netty, so every time I was going to ride Wolfie, I rode Netty first so I could loosen myself up before I got onto him.

My Cerebral Palsy makes me very stiff, particularly in my hips. Though it's important for certain parts of my body, such as my core, to be strong, there has to be a certain amount of relaxation. My seat and my hips need to remain soft and relaxed to allow both the movement of the horse through my body as well as allowing my thoughts, my signals to get through to the horse. If my hips are tight, then the messages can become blocked both ways.

It takes me 10 to 15 minutes to loosen myself up so we decided to carry out this process on Netty. By the time I got onto Wolfie, I would be relaxed and ready to focus on our training.

At this stage it was important my time on Wolfie was consolidated. It was better for us to have short but positive sessions rather than long drawn out ones. Because he was young everything needed to be of benefit to him as he was still learning.

By Autumn 2014, the hard work and perseverance from everyone involved was starting to pay off. A ridden partnership between Wolfie and I was developing nicely.

As part of Wolfie's training, Sophie would take him to compete in able-bodied British dressage competitions to get him used to competing at different venues.

It was during these competitions where Wolfie's potential shone. At Novice and Elementary level, he was achieving plus 75% marks. He was a star. It was so exciting!

Everything was going so well and our futures looked bright and full of promise. Then the unthinkable happened.

It was December 2014, just a few days before Christmas, when Wolfie came in from the field lame on one of his hind legs. By coincidence, there happened to be a vet on the yard who was looking at another horse and was able to see Wolfie. The vet put Wolfie on box rest, which meant he was to remain in his stable where his movement could be restricted. He was also given a course of pain relief.

We monitored Wolfie over the Christmas period, but by the new year there appeared to be no improvement. Having said that, there was no sign of swelling or heat anywhere. During the first week of January our usual vet came out to see Wolfie on two occasions and carried out various examinations. By the Friday, the vet decided that, as nothing was conclusive, he would send Wolfie to a veterinary hospital.

On Monday, January 12th, Mum and I took Wolfie to the hospital, with a friend, Mark, who drove the lorry.. I was worried as I had a lame horse, but no obvious sign of why he was lame. When we arrived and Mark got Wolfie out of the lorry, I remember thinking what a relief it was to be at the hospital. Wolfie was in the right place now.

We took Wolfie into the hospital where he was examined by a vet, who was a lameness specialist. Originally, Wolfie was meant to be having a scan, but we were told he wouldn't be able to have one until the following week. The vet examined Wolfie and the veterinary nurse trotted him up numerous times for the vet to look at him.

The vet then decided to nerve block him. Nerve blocking is where a local anaesthetic is injected, either close to a nerve or into a joint. If the horse has pain in the area which has been nerve blocked, the nerve block will temporarily numb it and the lameness will disappear. Wolfie had a series of nerve blocks in his right hind leg. Throughout the process I asked the vet, on several occasions, if he was going to x-ray Wolfie, to which he replied he didn't know which part of the leg to x-ray.

Eventually, to my relief, the vet decided he would x-ray. At this point, I was hugely relieved. At last they were investigating deeper. I stood back out of the way with Mum. I didn't want to get in the way, I just wanted them to get on with it.

My relief soon vanished. No sooner had the vet and nurse taken Wolfie into the x-ray room, they were bringing him back out again and taking him outside. All I wanted was for them to x-ray, even if it meant x-raying his whole leg.

Mum and I followed on, but as I am slower to walk, by the time I got out to them to ask what they were doing, it was too late. I saw them lunging Wolfie on the concrete and, as I got closer, Wolfie's hind leg shot out from underneath him. It was horrifying. Even today, I have that awful image in my mind. I knew straight away this was serious.

Wolfie was taken back into x-ray, where they x-rayed his lower leg, but it was too little, too late. By lunging him on the hard ground, this had caused his pastern (the joint above his hoof) to completely shatter. I went with the vet into the x-ray room and saw the x-ray. I was horrified to see the extent of the damage. It was like his pastern was in hundreds of pieces.

My mind was in complete turmoil. I am no vet, but even I could see it was devastation. The vet told me this could not be repaired. I could not believe what was happening. I remember suggesting to Mum we should get a second opinion, but then I couldn't help but think Wolfie would have been in so much pain, so was it fair to prolong his agony? I couldn't bear that thought. My beautiful, kind-hearted boy.

I went up to Wolfie to say goodbye. I was heartbroken.

I will forever be grateful to Mark for being there. He stayed with Wolfie whilst he was put to sleep. I went outside and sobbed. I could not believe what had just happened. Eventually we went home. The two-hour journey was awful, neither Mum, Mark or I spoke a word. We were all in utter shock. I stared out of the window. I felt numb.

The next few days were so tough. I just cried and cried. I didn't sleep for at least two days. The first few days I was grieving, but then my grief turned to anger and questioning. Questioning the vet's actions - why didn't he just x-ray him? Then questioning my actions - why wasn't I more insistent on him being x-rayed? I felt guilty and I did for a long, long time. I didn't protect my boy. I blamed myself. If only I had been more insistent on them x-raying at the beginning.

Saying goodbye to my special, baby boy was heartbreaking and the circumstances that led to his death on that day made it even worse. I think, without exaggerating, I cried for Wolfie every day for the first year.

After I lost my dad, I always said you never get over the loss of someone and the grief that it causes, but instead you learn to live with it, and it was the same after I lost Wolfie. I think about Wolfie every single day, but it is only relatively recently that I have felt a sense of acceptance.

This wonderful horse gave me so much love and sense of achievement in such a short space of time. He turned 'can't' into 'CAN' and for that I will be eternally grateful.

R.I.P Wolfie - my Special Boy X

CHAPTER 15
CRASHING, NETTY AND NEW OPPORTUNITIES

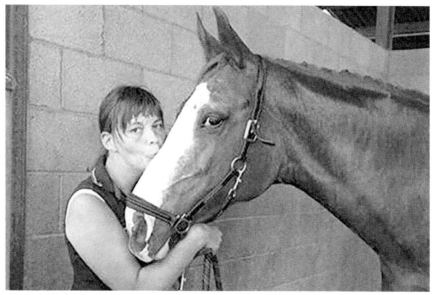

Summer 2016: I share a soppy moment with Donna Charisma before competing at Hartpury college.

oming to terms with Wolfie's death took a long, long time. Thanks to his amazing temperament in the stable, I had bonded with him more than I had done with any horse before, perhaps even Eddie.

For a time, I did consider giving up. I had experienced what mattered - it wasn't the competitions or the gold medals, but the horses. Nothing mattered anymore. I didn't care for squad or my team place, it wasn't about that, it was about my relationship with my horse and grieving for what I had lost.

It would have been easy to have stayed in that place, if it hadn't been for Netty.

Netty was a key member of my team. She had helped me develop the skills needed to be able to ride and get to grips with Wolfie.

After Wolfie's death, Netty's role in my life grew even more.

It was thanks to her that I ventured back on to the yard and started riding again. Just four days after I lost Wolfie, my friend, Emma, picked me up and took me to the yard. Fortunately, Netty's stable was the opposite end of the yard to Wolfie's, meaning I could head straight to her without having to pass what would have been Wolfie's home. It was a small, but important thing, as I battled with my emotions that day. I felt so lost without him and, for a short time, I no longer felt I belonged on the yard without my boy.

Despite the grief and sense of loss, within a couple of weeks, I started to ride Netty again. It was hard, but thanks to Netty, her owner Val and the support from Angela and the girls on the yard, I was able to get back to riding relatively quickly. Looking back, I think that I needed to. It was the best kind of healing for me.

Netty is amazing so let me tell you a bit more about her! She's 16.2hh and dark in colour and has the most gentle temperament. She's got a massive heart. However, nothing gets in the way of Netty and her food. She loves her carrots and will start 'talking' as soon as the bag of carrots come out.

When it comes to putting her head collar on, she can't possibly tear herself away from the hay net. Therefore, nowadays, my first challenge in a morning before I muck her out is to put her head collar on whilst her head is stuck in her hay net.

I always say she is not at all a 'girly girl' when it comes to affection and trying to give her a hug, it's like she's saying 'get off, don't be so soppy, get a grip!' With such a great temperament, I have been able to carry on doing with her the things I was able to do with Wolfie, such as grooming and putting her head collar and boots on ready to ride.

I christened Netty, 'Grandma Netty' as, emotionally, she has looked after me. She was my rock after I lost Wolf and when I was taken off the squad. From the riding point of view she has taught me so, so much!

Val, very kindly, said I could compete Netty to get me back into the competition arena and keep me on the competition scene.

Having this opportunity was great because it meant I could keep riding and competing. As I wasn't aiming for any team places on Netty, I could afford to focus on me and my riding without the worry of achieving selection criteria. This time was invaluable. I embraced the chance to learn and develop myself as a rider.

I soon learned that, despite previous protests with my trainers, they were right all along when they told me something changes in me as soon as the bell rings to begin my test. Having the opportunity to ride Netty in a test situation, it didn't take long to realise that as soon as the bell rang my brain went into 'test mode' and my body went tight. No wonder I couldn't ride a straight centre line or a square halt (in the halt, each leg forms a perfect square - a hoof at each corner).

Exactly the same can be said for riding Netty at home. Because of Netty's fantastic nature it meant that I could and still can ride Netty on my own without any supervision. This has been a massive achievement.

There was a time at the other yard when I used to ride Eddie on my own. However, one day I scared myself. It was windy and, whilst riding, I suddenly got it into my head, what if Eddie were to spook? I was on my own and, because I am not able to dismount on my own, I was stuck. I shouted for help but, as it was so windy, nobody heard me. To begin with I couldn't attract anybody's attention. I suddenly had the stark realisation that if Eddie got upset I wouldn't be able to do anything to get myself out of trouble.

Therefore, when I ride Netty now, I always take precautions and assess the situation before getting on.

Netty has given me the wonderful opportunity to work on me and my riding. I have been able to develop my ability to assess things, such as my position. From there I have learnt to work things out for myself and make my own decisions about the necessary adjustments I need to make.

I suppose the biggest and most valuable thing Netty has taught me is just how powerful the mind is and, how and to what extent the mind affects the body. Up until this point, Angela had always said I 'try too hard' and that I needed to ride with more 'thought' and less 'physical effort'.

Whilst riding on my own I experimented with this. I started to introduce my 'thinking' more, along with using correct breathing and relaxation. I soon began to realise just how influential 'thought' and 'breathing' was in achieving relaxation and harmony within the work.

This realisation has helped with my riding and day-to-day life and mental health. I have learned that if I have an ache or pain in my body there is probably something going on in my head and, nine times out of 10, this is the case.

I totally believe that, combined with Angela's training, Netty has helped me become a much better rider and for that I will be forever grateful.

A few months on from Wolfie's death and I could look to the future once again. Now I was in a better frame of mind to make decisions. It became apparent that, deep down, I did want to continue in my career. I was still desperate to get that paralympic gold medal, therefore I decided to look for another horse.

After searching the length and breadth of the country and a few false starts, I went to see a horse in the New Forest. This horse had come through David Hamer and been offered for loan to a para rider.

Donna Charisma was a very eye-catching 14-year-old chestnut mare. Just like Wolfie, she also had very good breeding and a super over-track in her walk.

After Angela, Sophie and I had been to see her in Somerset, we decided to give her a go. Charisma came home a few weeks later.

Like Wolfie, Charisma was a 'quality' horse. Although I didn't have the same 'wobbly' issues I had with Wolfie, she was quite a sensitive horse and brought about a whole new set of challenges. These challenges would further my education as a rider.

I started to compete Charisma over the winter of 2015/2016 and we were beginning to achieve some good results. So much so that we were selected to represent Great Britain at an international competition in Deauville, France in the March of 2016.

About two weeks before we were due to go to Deauville, Charisma and I competed at the Para Winter Championships at Vale View Equestrian Centre in Leicestershire.

Everything was fine until our test in the indoor arena. Then a quad bike started up and began to harrow the outside warm-up arena, running alongside the indoor arena.

Poor Charisma could hear the quad bike but couldn't see it. It spooked her and made her jump. Nothing major - she just jumped forward and then stopped. Although I lost my balance and fell forward a bit, my improved core strength meant I could stop her, re-adjust myself in the saddle, give Charisma a pat to reassure her and carry on with my test - no big deal.

To me, this wasn't an issue at all. Quite simply, Charisma spooked at something completely legitimate, but then composed herself, as did I, and we finished our test.

So, imagine my complete amazement, whilst at squad training, when I was pulled to one side by the squad manager and told that, because of Charisma's "behaviour" we were being withdrawn from the competition in Deauville.

I was so upset. The way in which my de-selection from Deauville was handled was appalling. I was told they would 'prefer it' that I didn't say anything to Angela until we got home. This put me in an extremely difficult position. Not only did I want to tell Angela, not least because she was my trainer and had a right to know, but also because I needed her support.

They told me they didn't want Angela to know until we got home, knowing full-well she would question their decision, and they didn't want that. At the time, I didn't know what to do. I then had to sit through a meeting about Deauville so Angela didn't suspect anything. It was a horrible situation. I felt as though I was betraying her by not telling her straight away but I was worried about the repercussions if I went against what the Squad Manager had asked.

I told Angela about the decision and what had happened as soon as we got home. She was just as upset and confused as I was. We appealed the selectors' decision but it didn't make any difference.

The thing that upset us the most was that neither the selectors or the squad manager talked over their apparent concerns with Angela. Angela trained Charisma and I and knew us better than anyone so why didn't they ask her opinion? Angela was not only my trainer but also a well-respected squad coach, yet her input, her experience and knowledge wasn't respected enough to be part of this decision. Appalling.

I still don't fully understand what went on.

As if this wasn't enough to deal with, in October 2016, the squad manager came to do a home visit and informed me I was being taken off the World Class Performance Squad. My contract would come to an end in January 2017.

Once again I was devastated. It felt as if during the time I was bringing home gold medals for the squad and my country everything was hunky-dory but, in the months and years after losing Wolfie, when I needed help and support, nothing was offered.

I often felt that, compared to other members of the squad, I didn't matter and yet I had achieved just like they had. There was a trust set up to buy horses for performance squad riders but I never understood why I was refused a trust horse.

At one point, shortly after Wolfie's death, there was a glimmer of hope. The squad coach told me the trust was going to buy me a horse. We even discussed how I went about finding one and how much money there was to spend. But then, just a few hours later, the squad coach told me I wasn't getting one. I couldn't believe it.

I never truly knew what their real opinion of Charisma was. When I asked for feedback I didn't get a satisfactory reply. I suppose, with my Deauville de-selection, I had found my answer.

I often wondered if they had their doubts about Charisma, why didn't they say? I could have then done something about it.

I was meant to have the support of World Class until my contract ended in the January. However, other than some contact with a lifestyle coach from the English Institute Of Sport, I heard nothing. My departure from the squad was meant to be announced within the equestrian world and in equestrian press but nothing ever happened (not that that worried me). I honestly felt as though I didn't matter. It was a horrible time and a horrible feeling to carry.

It wasn't long after I had learned of my departure from the squad that reality hit. Without my squad and UK Sport funding, unless I could find sponsorship or a job, then it was over. I would have to say goodbye to my career and, more importantly, be forced to say goodbye to the horses I loved. Horses that had done so much good for me throughout my life. Put simply, I wouldn't be able to afford to keep them. It was another devastating blow, but a blow that wouldn't keep me down for long.

From the moment I knew I was off squad, I started looking and applying for jobs. I spent every waking hour searching Google potential career ideas or any way to make money. I would have done anything to stop Charisma going back to her owner.

I would think of ideas and frantically type them into the search engine to find out whether my idea would be physically possible, whether it required any qualifications or whether it would earn me enough money.

Ideas came thick and fast. One idea was that of a primary school teaching assistant, though I have no idea why. I enrolled on an open-college course for 'assisting teaching and learning in primary schools' and I spent a term, one day a week, at the local primary school to see whether this idea was realistic. Whilst I thoroughly enjoyed my time and met some lovely children, it wasn't me. Swapping animals / horses for children wasn't going to satisfy the life I wanted.

By March 2018, I knew my time being able to keep Charisma was running out. I was getting more and more stressed and desperate. Time was against me and I just didn't know what to do.

Then, in one last-ditch attempt to 'save' Charisma and 'save' my career I decided to fund myself to go over to France to compete in the para international in Deauville. It was likely the only way I was going to have any chance of getting back on squad and prove myself internationally.

As it happened, my friend Heather was also self-funding and driving herself over. She kindly agreed she would take Charisma to Deauville in her lorry. So, that's what we did. Heather, Mum, me and a groom all travelled in Heather's vehicle together.

Despite all our efforts, all our hoping, our results in Deauville were mixed. Looking back now, I think this was partially due to stress and being so determined to not only prove myself to squad but probably, and more importantly, to ensure Charisma had a fair chance. I wanted her to be able to prove all her doubters wrong.

During the journey home, deep down, I think I knew this was the end. This would be my last competition. However, the optimist in me clutched at straws. I still had Charisma and whilst I still had her, I believed there was still hope. So, I continued my frantic search for answers. During this time, I drove myself mad and, I think, drove everyone else mad too.

Despite weeks of desperate pleas for help to keep Charisma, my time was up. In the May Charisma went back to her owner.

I was so distraught I didn't go with Mum to take Charisma back. I think the idea of having me blubbering all the way to Somerset and back was too much to bare. So, Mum took Charisma back and Heather drove the lorry.

It sounds silly, but up until Mum left the house that morning, my brain was still going into overdrive, trying to come up with solutions so Charisma could stay. Finally, at 7:30am, Charisma began her trip back to Somerset. That day was horrendous.

Waking up the day after Charisma left - a Monday morning and the beginning of a new week - I just stared at the ceiling, thinking now what do I do? It felt as though everything had been taken away from me and I had nothing left.

My whole life for 13 years had revolved around my training and my horses and now everything had gone. No horses to look after or orga- nise things for, no career, no training sessions with Angela, no real need to go to the gym. In my mind, it felt like I had nothing to live for anymore.

If I am no longer an international para dressage rider then, who am I?

This awful situation led to a totally different challenge to get through. I had been through depression before but this time things were different. There were days I believed the only way I could make my pain go away was to end it all. I had lost my purpose so, what was the point in being here?

I was already on anti-depressants. I had been since I lost Dad. However, things got so bad I decided I needed some help and was lucky to find it from a nice counsellor.

What stopped me ending it all, you may ask?

Amidst the chaos going on inside my head, a little voice would question my thoughts. 'What if tomorrow is a better day?' 'what if there is an answer waiting around the corner?' Fortunately, it was this little voice that made me stay.

Ultimately, though I was in a depressive state, another side of me was desperate to try one last time to find a new purpose. I needed purpose, I needed to be something.

Then suddenly, one day, I found it - the answer I was looking for, and it was staring me right in the face!

CHAPTER 16

NEW AMBITIONS

A standing ovation at TEDxPeterborough in 2019 with my talk, There's No Such Word As Can't. Pic courtesy of Vicki Head Photography.

After a few weeks went by, I needed to get myself sorted. I needed to find a new purpose. I was adamant I was going to get my horses and career back. This new 'purpose' was just a 're-route' to help me get to my end goal, however long it would take me to achieve.

Whilst I sat searching Google for answers one day, I had a thought. In my years on the world class performance squad, I received National Lottery funding from UK Sport. Part of the contract meant athletes were required to go into schools, clubs, etc. to give motivational talks or presentations to encourage the next generation.

Prior to being on the performance squad I had dabbled in public or motivational speaking and I had the opportunity of speaking at some big events. My first ever speaking engagement was in 2005 when I was invited to deliver the final speech at the Riding for the Disabled Association's national conference at Lincolnshire showground. My audience was 250 RDA members and HRH Princess Anne, the charity's president.

It was this event where I shared the talk that formed the basis of the keynote speech I still deliver today, now entitled 'From Therapy to World Champion'.

Whilst speaking at the RDA conference I explained just how much riding had helped me - from when I was just two years old and my parents were told riding could really help my development, through the years riding with the RDA and then onto what, at that time, was my new challenge - para dressage.

I felt really, really nervous. This was not only my first ever speaking engagement, but I was speaking to a large audience and, to make the situation more nerve-racking, HRH Princess Anne was sitting right in front of me.

I needn't have worried. I received a standing ovation from the whole audience, including Princess Anne. Wow, I couldn't have been more proud!

This was an awesome feeling. I felt a great sense of pride and a real buzz.

After my speech, I was invited to have tea with Princess Anne. There were no heirs nor graces and she was extremely down to earth. Her passion for horses, riding and the RDA was clear to see, as was her wealth of knowledge. I was nervous about meeting and talking to her but our common interest of horses made the conversation easier. It flowed nicely and her sense of humour made me feel at ease.

During our time chatting, she congratulated me on my talk and we talked about my riding and future plans. I also had lots of positive feedback from many RDA members.

Following on from the RDA's national conference, a delegate who heard my talk invited me to deliver the same talk at a business conference for Kleeneze in 2006.

This audience was even bigger - 300 delegates! This seemed even scarier, although no royalty this time. Once again, my talk was very well received and, yet again, I was buzzing. It was an amazing feeling.

With these positive experiences under my belt, it suddenly occurred to me just how much I enjoyed delivering motivational talks and sharing my story. In that moment, I made the decision - I was going to market myself as a motivational speaker.

As with all key moments throughout my career, Mum was right there supporting me.

At this stage my family, and certainly Mum, could see this was a positive decision and a feasible option. I have been grateful for their support from day one. I am especially grateful for Mum's support. Now she often jokes she has swapped driving me all over the country with a horse to now driving me all over the country to speaking gigs.

My speaking career was beginning to blossom and it felt good. I had already had a booking to speak at Grantham Business Club's expo evening as their keynote speaker, so this was a good start. As a result of the talk, I was invited to attend a business networking event - 4Networking in Grantham.

After my first meeting, I decided to join 4N which would give me access to regular networking and plenty of business opportunities. It was whilst I was at this meeting that I met my mentor, Taz Thornton.

Taz was giving the 20 minute talk. When she walked into the room I was suddenly confronted with this pink-haired, loud (in a good way!) bundle of joy!

During the 40 second introduction round, I discovered Taz was a motivational speaker. I remember thinking 'perfect' and swiftly arranged a one-to-one meeting with her. After listening to her talk, I was so inspired I bought her book, Unleash Your Awesome and, despite my dislike for reading, read it. One chapter every night until I had finished it. Her book was very inspiring and helpful with the things I was going through at the time. I remember seeing Taz at another meeting and telling her she should feel honoured I was reading her book, given my distinct lack of interest in book reading up until this point.

Every time I met Taz at 4N meetings I would endeavour to get a one-to-one appointment as I wanted to learn from her.

Soon after my first 4N meeting I got some business cards printed and started marketing the two talks I had developed - 'From Therapy to World Champion' and 'There's No Such Word As Can't'.

'There's No Such Word As Can't' is still a popular talk I deliver today and I use this as a tagline for my business.

It was Spring 2018 when I asked Taz if she would mentor me. She now helps me to develop as a motivational speaker plus helps with marketing and developing my speaking into a business. Thanks to Taz, I have built up my confidence to be able to speak without notes and have a burgundy, navy and cream brand I am very proud of, with a tagline to match. I also have business cards, banners, talk backdrops and social media headers all on brand.

Taz not only mentors me in my business, but also in my mindset and, in recent times, has helped me out of some dark places. If I have any 'mental moments', then poor Taz gets it but then she often responds by giving me a good 'kick up the bum' when needed.

Taz and I get on really well. We both like a laugh but we also want to use our own experiences to help people. I think this is why we make such a good team!

It was through meeting Taz and her wife, Asha that I was invited to speak at my first TEDx event - TEDx Peterborough in April 2019. Asha was curator of the first ever TEDxPeterborough. I was extremely honoured and proud to be asked to speak at such a well-known event for speakers. It's great to know my TEDx talk is now being viewed across the globe on YouTube. At the time of writing, the TEDx YouTube channel had more than 22 million followers so a fantastic showcase for my work.

Speaking at TEDx was a new experience. The event was held in a theatre, which brought the audience closer and made the whole thing more intimate. It was amazing!

Once again I was nervous. This was a big event being recorded for YouTube and would also add weight to my motivational speaking CV. Therefore, it had to go well. I shared my story through 'There's No Such Word As Can't' which also included the challenges of my para dressage career coming to an unexpected end.

I was speechless when, after delivering my final line "… and I want to prove There is No Such Word As Can't"… everybody stood and gave me a standing ovation! I couldn't believe it!

I love motivational speaking, just as I will always love competing, and I have found the psychological effects are quite similar. After competing at big competitions, such as the World Equestrian Games and now, after speaking at events like TEDx, after the highs of adrenaline, I have fallen back down and into low mood. I suppose it's like bursting a balloon. It is during these times where I have had to use my mental strength to lift back up to baseline again.

Earlier in 2019, I was invited to speak at Brad Burton's (the founder of 4N) 'Now What Live' - a motivational event held at Aston Villa Football Club. I was also asked to speak at Ignite business conference in Bedfordshire, run by Kathryn Slack.

Speaking at these events, as well as having help and support from Taz, has been invaluable in my development as 'Emma Sheardown, TEDx/ Motivational Speaker and International Para Dressage Champion!'

I am now looking forward to developing my career as a motivational speaker. My ambition is to use my own experiences to promote disability awareness education and training. I am particularly interested in delivering this within the business sector, looking at the employment of people with disabilities and educating members of staff around interaction with disabled customers or clients. My goal is to be able to deliver this education to as many high street companies as I can.

I feel strongly about disability awareness, acceptance and inclusion. It makes me sad that there is so much stigma and discrimination in the world … and disability is just one of them. I will never understand why people have such a negative mindset, whether it be due to disability, race or sexual orientation … after all we are still 'one' human race.

Amongst those people who don't want to know about disability issues, are also those who simply don't understand and are too afraid of doing or saying the wrong thing. My aim is to help people to feel more confident about interacting and communicating with those who have disabilities.

I want to make people aware that "just because my legs don't work properly, it doesn't mean that my brain doesn't either" and that if they are prepared to be patient "listen, learn and let me show you what I can do!"

For me, if somebody is in doubt, then please ask! Don't assume I need help. If you ask I will be grateful for the offer. Please don't assume my Cerebral Palsy is accompanied by a cognitive disability - I hope that by reading this book you will have discovered this is definitely not the case.

And my ultimate goal? That's easy. To make my business a success and to be able to fund myself back into the saddle. I still have the same passion for horses and for dressage today that I had at the beginning of my competitive journey.

Although I am extremely lucky to have Netty to ride and I thoroughly enjoy helping out on the yard, I still have unfinished business – Paralympic Gold!

All those years ago, the day that I said "look Mummy, I can walk", I not only proved the medics wrong but I proved that I can! I will continue pushing boundaries and I suggest you do too.

Please, always remember that whatever other people say;

#TheresNoSuchWordAsCant

Emma

X

CHAPTER 17

EMMA: PAT'S STORY

Beside me all the way: Mum and I, 2020.

I was overjoyed to discover I was expecting my first baby. John already had three sons but he was thrilled to learn he was to be a dad again. I was 37 years old and was referred to as a 'matron mum'. I didn't feel at all matronly. I had always played sport, walked a lot and ate healthily.

So, to find myself two weeks overdue, needing an emergency caesarean section and having a baby brain damaged due to lack of oxygen to the brain caused through fetal distress wasn't something I had anticipated and never could have imagined.

Nor was having her christened at 38 hours old because she wasn't expected to survive the night, being told it was unlikely she would walk or talk and then facing years of physiotherapy, speech and occupational therapy along with all the uncertainty.

Our lives changed forever that day, Tuesday 29th January 1985.

I have cried many tears and asked myself over and over again how could this have happened – why did it happen?

But it did happen.

I had a problem free pregnancy, I didn't smoke or drink and I ate sensibly. So to get to the end of my pregnancy and then have problems was something I didn't expect or understand.

At each appointment with my obstetrician I was told I would not be allowed to go over my due date, 14th January. That date came and went. Two weeks later, during the evening of the 27th January I started to get a few spasmodic pains and felt uncomfortable. I had a bath and went to bed. During the early hours of Monday morning the pains got worse. I timed them but they were still spasmodic. I was advised to go to hospital.

On arrival I was examined but was assured nothing was happening. I stayed at the hospital and was monitored but, as the pains had stopped, I was told I could go home. This decision worried me. I was two weeks' overdue and was repeatedly told I wouldn't go over my time. I voiced my concerns and was eventually admitted and told I would be induced the next day. I persuaded John to go home and get some rest - easier said than done. He arrived back at the hospital early the next morning and was faced with a scene he could only describe as 'panic' and somehow he knew it involved me.

The procedure to induce me hadn't worked. I needed a caesarean section because the baby was distressed and both of our lives were at risk. Everything seemed to happen so quickly from then on. I can remember thinking 'I must keep calm for the sake of the baby' but, in reality, I was so worried. I can't remember anything else after that until John spoke to me in the recovery room and told me we had a daughter. The joy of having a daughter and the relief I felt quickly changed when the doctor told us she didn't breathe to start with and was transferred to the special baby care unit. I can't remember how long it took for her to breathe but sadly it was long enough to cause brain damage.

During that first day I didn't see Emma, other than on a photograph taken by the Sister on special care. However, my sisters, Christine and Barbara, were allowed to see her, but only through a glass partition.

This was an emotional time for them, especially Christine.

As a family, we couldn't believe this situation was happening again. In 1982 Christine gave birth prematurely to twin girls, Laura and Andrea. Sadly, Laura died at birth and Andrea survived for only two days. To see Emma fighting for her life brought so many emotions to the fore.

Christine said it was so upsetting to see Emma lying in a fetal position, wired to various monitors. She described her as having a bad, bluey colour but, most noticeable, were her tight fists. My other sister, Barbara, also noticed this.

I was taken to see Emma in the special baby care unit the next day. John went with me. What should have been such a happy moment seeing my baby for the first time, was heart breaking. I was only able to touch Emma through the side of the cot by holding her hand. She was sleeping and had monitors and wires connected to various parts of her body.

The moment was devastating and I truly believed she wouldn't live, she looked so lifeless. John and I needed each other so much at that moment. We couldn't speak, we just cried together. In all this turmoil, a nurse wanted me to express milk for Emma. I managed to, but how? I don't know. I think at that moment I would have done anything to help her.

I was in a side ward - part of the main ward where the mums with new babies were. The only way I could get to see my baby was if someone took me. I was on the middle floor and the special baby care unit was on the top floor.

I could hear what was going on in the ward. Mums talking and laughing, babies crying - something I should have been part of but I didn't feel like laughing or talking. It broke my heart hearing those babies crying when I didn't know if my baby was going to live. I wanted to believe she would survive but deep down I didn't think she would.

I didn't want to go on the main ward all tearful. I didn't want to put a dampner on everyone else's happiness but I found it very difficult to put on a brave face. I guess they found it very difficult to be around me too. There were two mums, who I knew and whose babies were born the day after Emma, who came to see me. I appreciated that.

During the early hours of the Thursday morning doctors feared Emma wasn't going to make it. She was about 38 hours old. They phoned John and asked him if we wanted her christened and to confirm her name. The priest had already been called and John was told to get to the hospital quickly if he wanted to see her christened, it was that urgent.

On arrival, John had difficulty getting into the hospital as the doors were locked. Luckily, he found a porter who let him in and he made it just in time to see her christened. He stayed with her until the doctor told him Emma was holding her own and suggested he went home and got some sleep.

He told me he went home and laid in front of the Rayburn, distraught and cuddling a toy lamb. I was so pleased my sisters went to see him and gave him support.

At some time between 1am and 2am, I went to the bathroom. On returning, I sat on my bed and, for some unknown reason, looked at the vase of flowers on the bedside cabinet. Why I thought there were some flowers missing I don't know, but I was sure there were. I thought no more of it but later the sister came into my ward carrying some flowers. They had been taken during the night for Emma's christening.

I didn't know Emma wasn't expected to survive the night or John had been called in. I don't know whose decision it was not to wake me, other than it was a medical one. I was so upset about it. I should have been there for Emma and John as well as me. I often think what would have happened if she had died that night and I wasn't there.

Knowing Emma had got through the night, both my sisters thought she had probably turned the corner.

John was so worried she wasn't going to make it that he rang my friend Brit and asked her to come over from Aldridge in the West Midlands.

During that day, it was still touch and go. We didn't know whether she would make it. I sat with her for what seemed like hours talking and praying for her to live. I had only held her twice up to this time but it was such an amazing experience and I couldn't visualise her not being with us. We got through the day.

Do you believe in miracles?

I believe miracles happen because from that day Emma began to improve. It was slow progress and she was still on various monitors, especially the heart monitor. Breast feeding was very slow and seemed to take forever, but we persevered.

After six days, I was discharged, but able to stay in the parent's accommodation so I could be with Emma. John would come and spend time with her so I could rest. I was still recovering from my caesarean. As each day arrived, doctors were pleased with Emma's progress. John and I could hold her more often and for longer periods of time. Gradually they removed all the tubes until she was completely free of them. At last I could bath her on my own, without having to worry about disconnecting anything.

At 10 days old, we got the news we had been waiting for. We could take Emma home. I thought we would never see that day so tears of sadness turned to tears of joy.

During those first few weeks we had regular visits from the midwife. Breast feeding was a problem so we changed to the bottle and from then on feeding became routine. I suppose everything else eventually became routine. During those early months I had amazing support from my sisters and my mum.

We then had regular visits to see the heart specialist and at three-months-old Emma was discharged from hospital care.

As Emma got older, my mum and sisters could see she wasn't developing as she should. They thought I was closing my eyes to the situation but I think I was looking for different signs of development that weren't there. John thought she was 'just slow'.

However, we had to acknowledge that, because she couldn't roll over or show signs of sitting up, we needed to see our GP and voice our concerns. Emma would be about 10 months old at this point. Our

GP told us, because we were older parents, we were being over protective. However, we did convince him to start the ball rolling and
referred us to the paediatrician at Grantham Hospital.

We were then referred to see a specialist at Nottingham City
Hospital. This was the start of a number of appointments so they could
do various tests. These tests included physiotherapy, speech and occupational therapy and were done on a regular basis for approximately
three months. She also had a lumbar puncture, brain scans and x-rays.

We were eventually told Emma had Cerebral Palsy and that her
future was uncertain. She was 14 months old and she probably wouldn't
walk or talk.

I remember the day quite clearly. It was a morning appointment
at Nottingham City Hospital and, after receiving the news, we had to
wait to have more x rays in the afternoon. We passed the time between
appointments walking around the hospital grounds. Going through my
head were the words 'Cerebral Palsy, probably won't walk or talk'. John
and I were in complete shock, so much so that we walked in silence. What
did it all mean? There we were pushing Emma around in her pushchair,
she was wide awake, smiling and full of life. How could this be?

When my sisters and friend, Brit learnt of Emma's diagnosis they
did some research and quickly realised we were facing a difficult time.
We would need all the support available. To this day they have been
there every step of the way and have seen Emma become the amazing
person she is today.

Sadly, my mum passed away shortly after Emma's diagnosis so
wouldn't see her granddaughter grow up.

John was so proud of all Emma achieved. He supported her in
everything she did and would, like me, be extremely proud of everything
she's doing today. Like him she's a worker, but she' a fighter too.

Pat Sheardown

CHAPTER 18
MY HORSES

Netty, my best friend and 'rock'. September 2018.

Slightly Welton (Spider)

S adly, since leaving my old yard in 2012 and the circumstances surrounding my departure, I am no longer in contact with Spider. However, I understand Spider is still owned by the lady I sold him to. Since then he has helped many riders in the riding school where I learnt to ride and this also includes working with RDA riders.

Purdy's Dream (Eddie)

Eddie has enjoyed the past five years living with new owners, Claire and daughter Chloe. I was extremely lucky to find my 'Golden Boy' such lovely new owners.

Heartbreakingly, Eddie passed away during the editing of this book - in February 2020. He was 22 years old.

RIP Golden Boy - Thank you for making my dreams come true.

Donna Charisma

After Charisma went back to her owner, Lorna Davis, in 2017, Lorna found Charisma a lovely new home with a young rider and her family, giving her new rider experience as well as the opportunity to compete.

Sadly, during the writing of this book, Donna Charisma developed a degenerative condition in her joints and sadly passed away in September 2019, just two months after I had been to visit her at her new home in Somerset.

RIP x

Netty

Netty celebrates her milestone birthday in 2020 as she reaches the grand age of 30.

She enjoys a quieter life now, providing therapy riding for adults and children with disabilities at Papplewick RDA in Nottinghamshire. Having said that, she is still enthusiastic when I ride her - still keen to work and continues to teach me so much.

CHAPTER 19

TEACHERS FOR ALL OF US

Every medal won is a tribute to the support team – two legs and four legs – that helped me win.

You know, animals are smart.... they are *really* smart! I feel very honoured to have been surrounded by them my whole life - from dogs, to sheep, to horses.

The thing I have found fascinating over the years is that animals seem to know when something is not quite right, or different, in some way.

Growing up on the family farm, we had a sheepdog called Boss. Boss would come bounding up to me, then he would just stop. He would put the brakes on, just in front of me... it was as if he knew he mustn't jump up in case I fell over.

My World and European championship horse, Eddie, looked after me to a whole new level. On several occasions, something made Eddie jump. If horses get spooked, they'll often shoot off; they are flight animals and, if something frightens them, their natural instinct is to run.

Eddie was different.

Yes, he would naturally jump at the thing that startled him and I would fall onto his neck, but then he would stop... it was as if he knew instinctively that I was vulnerable and had to look after me.

When you think about it, Eddie's intuition to look after me somehow replaced his natural instincts. How extraordinary was that?

I've been blessed to work with so many fantastic animals over the years and each one has taught me so much.

They have been wonderful teachers for me. I hope they are for you too.

CHAPTER 20

ONE FINAL THOUGHT

Anybody who is perceived as being 'different' within society is very sadly at risk of prejudice. I wish I knew why. I don't understand… why can't people accept we are one human race?

Whether we are black or white, love another person of the same sex or have a disability, we are all human, so why on earth can't people accept that and live peacefully side by side?

When it comes to disability awareness and acceptance, I am in no way saying people aren't cruel because they are. People say or do things that can truly hurt but I also think people are genuinely fearful of doing or saying the wrong thing.

People that have a fear and don't know how to react on meeting a person with a disability generally want to be inclusive but they just don't know how.

I honestly believe those people do try to look at the person and not the disability but they are confronted by barriers of uncertainty.

These barriers may send an array of questions in their head about the best way to interact with the disabled person and it is these questions that hold them back.

"What do I say?" "Can he talk?" "Does she understand?"

I do understand this. It is a difficult one as you don't want to upset the person you are communicating with. Neither do you want to find yourself in an awkward or embarrassing situation.

I want to encourage you to be brave and say 'hello'.

You may feel a little apprehensive as you wait for a reply and this is where you must open your mind to other methods of communication.

It maybe they have a communication aid such as an iPad, like me, they need time and patience whilst they get their words out or perhaps communication is by facial expressions — giving a simple smile for 'yes' and a grumpy face for 'no'.

"Do I help?" may also be a question you are faced with. The simple answer to this is please ask! If you watch me struggle to put my coat on you might feel like jumping in and helping me but please don't. I appreciate any offer of help but I also need the opportunity to try myself.

So, if you want to offer your help, let us have a conversation.

The opposite of people with good intentions who want to help and understand are the people who are discriminatory, who are cruel and who just don't want to know.

For these people I am referring to, sadly inclusion and equality don't matter. To them we are different, our disabilities are a freak of nature — they don't see the person underneath the disability.

These people stare at me, they snigger when I wobble around — I am sure they think I am drunk!

The time and patience I often talk about… well that's a joke! These members of society haven't got time to wait around for me, they are in too much of a rush to hold the heavy door open for me to wobble through, they haven't got time to stop and wait to hear what I have got to say and they see me as being completely different to them.

So, let me show you, I am really no different to you!

My legs might not work like yours, I might stumble around like a bull in a china shop and you might think I talk 'funny'… but I am still a human being, a human being just like you.

Just like you I have feelings, emotions, hopes, dreams and ambitions. My brain might affect the way in which my muscles work but there's absolutely nothing wrong with my intelligence…

Go on, let's have a conversation about it. I may need more time to get my words out but I promise it's well worth the wait!

I truly hope you have enjoyed reading this book and taking the journey with me.

If you have, I'd love you to write a review on www.Amazon.co.uk, please – it will help encourage others to read There's No Such Word As Can't and, of course, you'll encourage me to write more too!

I'd also love to hear from you direct. If you'd like to get in touch, please email Emma@EmmaSheardown.com

You can catch up with me on social media too.

Follow me on

Twitter: @Sheardown_Emma

Facebook: https://www.facebook.com/ESheardownMotivationalSpeaker/

LinkedIn: https://www.linkedin.com/in/esheardown-motivationalspeaker/

ACKNOWLEDGEMENTS

Writing this book has been a fantastic reminder of how many people have been involved in sharing this amazing journey with me and supported me in making my achievements possible.

I could never have envisaged myself doing this and I have found it to be a cathartic experience as I have re-lived the highs and lows, the fun times, the desperate times and the achievements and disappointments.

There are so many people I need to thank for contributing to my story and the piecing together of this book:

Mum

Thank you for being my rock, believing in me and never giving up right from day one. From the day I was diagnosed with Cerebral Palsy, Mum committed herself to various daily therapy programmes to get me as well and physically able as she could. Her dedication was rewarded when, aged six, I took my first steps unaided.

Throughout my life Mum has committed herself 100 per cent to supporting me down my chosen paths and to achieving my goals. She has made her own sacrifices to enable me to achieve.

Mum has played a huge part in the writing of this book, not least in sharing her own story.

Asha Clearwater

I thank Asha so much for helping me make this the book it is today.

When I handed her the first draft it was a shadow of what it is now. By asking questions and getting me to dig a bit deeper, she has helped me expand and develop my story. Her hard work and dedication has helped me piece together the memories and achievements which prove 'There's No Such Word As Can't'.

My Family

During the early years of my life, my family played an important role in my development, often getting involved in therapy programmes to give Mum and Dad a break. Likewise, they were always there to support them when things were tough. Thank you for supporting me on my journey.

Therapists

To all the therapists involved in my early years development, thank you. Thanks for your commitment and specialist knowledge that enabled me to defy the predictions of the medical profession by getting me walking and talking.

To my physiotherapist, Liz Kendall, for her suggestion of horse riding as a therapy. Who would have known it would lead to the amazing career it did? Thank you.

Angela Weiss

Thank you for turning me into the rider I always wanted to be.

For her time, patience, knowledge and dedication that allowed me to develop as a rider and form the important partnerships I was so lucky to experience with my horses.

Angela was influential in my achievements in becoming European and world champion… something which I will forever be grateful for.

And to Angela's mum and dad for all their support and encouragement during some of the most challenging moments in my life.

Taz Thornton

I can't thank Taz enough for everything she has done for me. From coaching me in my new career as a motivational speaker, helping me to grow my business and playing a big part in creating the brand I have today, the brand I am proud of.

Taz has also been there through some of my darkest moments, giving me the support and tools needed to dig myself out of those lowest points and get me back on track.

I don't know where I would be without Taz's kick up the bum.

My Horses

Where do I start? These extraordinary creatures have played such a huge part in my life.

From therapy, to filling me with passion for my sport … and eventually onto achieving in a career I never thought possible.

More importantly, they gave me compassion, connection and more joy, achievement and pride than I could ever imagine.

From little Dusty Bin to 17.1hh Eddie, each one has played a significant part in my story... and for each one I will forever be grateful.

You

Thank you for picking up my book and reading it. Wow, I can't put into words how much this means to me!

I hope you enjoy it and that a little piece of my story positively impacts you in some way.

The main thing I would love you to take away from the book is that whatever life throws at you, whatever challenges you face, in the rollercoaster of life:

There's No Such Word As Can't

Emma

X